MARK JAMES WALSH

Hire without Recruitment Agencies

MARK JAMES WALSH

Copyright © 2014 Mark James Walsh
All rights reserved.

LIMIT OF LIABILITY / DISCLAIMER OF WARRANTY

This publication has been written to provide general information and advice with regard to the subject matter and is presented with no implied warranty or guarantee of any kind. The strategies and advice contained herein are based upon the professional experience of the author and may not be suitable for every situation. You should always seek legal or professional advice where appropriate. The author shall not be held liable for any commercial damages resulting from the use of information contained within this publication. No part of this publication may be reproduced, stored or transferred other than for personal use without the express permission of the author.

HIRE WITHOUT RECRUITMENT AGENCIES

CONTENTS

1	Stop Wasting Money on Recruitment Fees	Pg 1
2	Candidate Sourcing	Pg 14
3	How to find passive candidates	Pg 42
4	Developing a talent pool	Pg 55
5	How to read and shortlist CVs	Pg 61
6	Spreading the hiring message	Pg 75
7	Interviewing – getting the most of the process	Pg 81
8	Managing the offer process	Pg 102
9	Making the most of the closing process	Pg 115
10	Making it happen with the ten key steps in your action plan	Pg 128

Introduction

The recruitment of new staff frequently turns into a fruitless, time consuming and wasteful process much to the annoyance of all involved. Without clearly defining exactly what you need and making sure to get the input of all the decision makers up front means the process can very easily go wrong. Often you cannot find suitable candidates or the perfect candidate comes along and at the end of the process rejects your offer leaving you right back where you started.

Working with a recruitment agency can sometimes help, although, it is an expensive option. I would strongly argue that agencies do not operate with your interests at heart. Why would they when they simply exist to produce revenue month on month. Most agency recruiters are specifically measured on monthly income, not efficiency, not their levels of repeat business or the quality of placements they make. Agencies exist solely to produce steady monthly revenue streams. If your vacancy can't be filled either this month or next then they're not really going to be focused on filling it. The recruitment industry is filled with people looking to make placements as quickly as possible in order to meet their own personal fee targets.

A typical recruitment process takes place over a period of two to four weeks but normally only involves somewhere between twelve and twenty four hours of actual work. This would usually involve advertising and sourcing candidates, reading CVs, short-listing possible candidates, arranging interviews and possibly assisting the offer process for the final successful candidate. Each step involves a certain amount of administrative activities. Communicating and giving regular updates to all involved also takes up a certain amount of time. According to some of the leading players in the general recruitment market in the UK such as online Jobs Board Monster, HR Magazine, The Recruitment and Employment Federation and The Chartered Institute of Personnel Development the cost of filling a vacancy using a recruitment agency averages in the £4,000 - £5,000 region per hire. Check out the links below for further info.

http://hiring.monster.co.uk/hr/hr-best-practices/recruiting-hiring-advice/managing-hiring-costs/what-are-the-general-costs-of-using-recruitment-agencies.aspx

https://www.rec.uk.com/news-and-policy/press-releases/uk-recruitment-market-set-to-surpass-pre-recession-peak-by-the-end-of-201314-rec

http://www.hrmagazine.co.uk/hro/news/1020605/talent-aquistion-costs-rise-uk-gbp5-311-hire-compared-gbp2-226-us

http://www.cipd.co.uk/binaries/recruitment_retention_turnover_annual_survey_2009.pdf

HIRE WITHOUT RECRUITMENT AGENCIES

So, you are therefore typically paying hundreds of Euros or Pounds per hour for the work that is carried out on your behalf with no real guarantee of success in terms of hiring a suitable candidate. The actual work involved requires no real specialist skills. It could be carried out by the vast majority of businesses by themselves for a fraction of the cost and often to higher standards than those achieved by most recruitment agencies.

An average agency recruiter needs to spend a significant amount of his or her time chasing new business and completing administrative tasks. That leaves a limited amount of time available to do what you're paying them to do – finding and engaging with suitable candidates that you would like to interview. The competitive nature of today's market means your average recruiter will have to work on something like ten jobs per week and will probably fill no more than one job per week. The nine jobs that don't get filled will still involve about one to two hours work each even though there is no fee payable to them for that work. The amount of their time spent on revenue generating activities is quite small and this contributes to the overall high cost of using their services. Because of this inefficiency, when they do make a successful placement they tend to be quite expensive. They need to be in order for their employers to stay in business! The fees they receive for the jobs that they do manage to fill are required to pay for all the time they must spend chasing new business and working on roles that they don't manage to fill – it's basically a gamble for agency recruiters in terms of where they invest their time.

Mark Walsh Profile

Mark has spent over ten years earning a successful living in the hiring business. He is a committed problem solver and enjoys implementing real-world solutions. He has earned a reputation for solving difficult recruitment problems that others shy away from or have given up on.

Mark started life as a materials engineer having graduated with a BSc (honours) in Polymer Technology in 1994 and spent almost ten years in the automotive manufacturing sector. Since moving into the "people" business in 2003 he has gained a Post Grad in Business Administration and the Project Management Institute's PMP certification.

He has worked on both sides of the fence, directly with clients and with recruitment agencies and so has a deep understanding of how the recruitment industry operates. He has managed recruitment teams and projects for challenging engineering projects in international environments. He has personally been responsible for the hiring of over one thousand professionals. He has spent over ten thousand hours conducting interviews and has read well over one hundred thousand CVs in his career to date.

He has learned that whatever your hiring needs your best chance of success is through the use of a systematic approach. A strong focus on high quality communications with all parties involved is essential. A clear plan and clearly communicated objectives will maximise your chances of success in finding and hiring the right people for your business.

CHAPTER 1: STOP WASTING MONEY ON RECRUITMENT FEES

Recruitment Agencies – the truth and the myths

Recruitment agencies saw massive growth in the 1980s and today they play a huge part in the modern business world. Revenues reached an all time peak of £27 billion in 2008 in the UK market according to The Recruitment and Employment Federation:

https://www.rec.uk.com/news-and-policy/press-releases/uk-recruitment-market-set-to-surpass-pre-recession-peak-by-the-end-of-201314-rec

Most agencies operate on the basis of an introduction fee. Fees vary widely from ten percent for the lowest level high street agency to thirty percent or more for the specialist boutique type. Most agencies operate in the 15 to 25 percent bracket and will offer varying service levels ranging from little more than a shortlist of CVs into your inbox right up to a fully managed service culminating in the successful offer and placement of a candidate.

Now I'm not saying that all agencies offer bad value for money but I am saying that they are only really useful in certain situations. Furthermore they are over used as the default option by far too many businesses. Why businesses routinely pay agencies thousands to find people for them never ceases to amaze me. This work could be done in house for a fraction of the cost and also to a higher standard. I know this because I have spent over ten years hiring engineers and managers for clients while working both as an in-house recruiter and as a recruitment agency consultant.

When should you use a recruitment agency?

- When you need to discreetly or confidentially source potential candidates and you cannot publicly advertise vacancies.

- When you are looking to head hunt senior people directly and they are unlikely to be actively looking for a new role.

- When you have an immediate short-term urgent need that necessitates a temporary hire or a contractor with very specific skills.

When you know that a particular recruitment agency has suitable candidates on their books then they will certainly be of use to you. If they have the ability to contact the type of candidates you need they can also provide a very useful service. If neither of the above is true then the odds of an agency being able to help you are quite small. So if most jobs can be filled with only twenty four hours work without any real specialist training or skills why not do it in-house where you can cut the cost and improve the quality?

Things you should be aware of when using a recruitment agency

Recruitment agencies provide an introduction service. They get paid for introducing a person to you by sending you the CV of that person. By requesting an interview you are agreeing to their terms and conditions and engaging the agency as your supplier. They may not have sent you anything to sign and you may not be aware of the small print on the CV or the email directing you to their terms. Terms and conditions can often be printed at the bottom of the CV in very small print. They can be included as a footnote in an email signature or there can be a link to the terms contained on the agency website. A lot of people proceed to interview and indeed make candidate offers without thinking about what the costs will be. They then get a shock when it's explained that they've already agreed to terms and they discover what the fee is. The fee is due simply for the introduction, nothing else. By asking the agency to set up an interview you are engaging them and you will also likely be inadvertently agreeing to their terms.

> Tip - Always seek clarification of agency terms and conditions before interviewing any candidates. By requesting an interview you may actually be accepting their standard terms and conditions.

In the event of things going wrong and a candidate not working out as hoped, most agencies do not offer a refund but rather a replacement candidate instead. At this stage you've already parted with your money so they are often a lot less committed to making a placement second time around. It's very rare for anybody to get a refund from an agency. One trick that's frequently used as a get-out clause is the payment terms. Most agency terms state that invoices must be paid within a very short time period, one or two weeks, knowing full well they won't be paid on time as very few companies operate their payment processes to such short deadlines. By paying late you've voided your right to a free replacement and they are therefore under no obligation should a candidate not work out.

Most agency terms will also state that you, the client, are solely responsible for verifying the suitability of the person for the job. This includes their legal right to do the job, their medical fitness and pretty much everything else. What I'm basically driving at here is the fact that agencies are really only providing an introduction service of somebody who might be what you need. The decision and all associated risk is therefore yours.

If you allow different agencies to compete over the same roles you thereby add another dimension. Each agency is duty bound to forward any and all CVs of people that you might consider hiring in case their competition does it before them. This is a cardinal sin for any recruiter. It looks very bad for an agency recruiter if one of their candidates is placed into a job by a rival agency. Such events inevitably lead to a stern talking to from senior management. I'm trying to paint a picture here of the kind of pressures recruiters are under to fill jobs quickly and then move on to the next placement.

It's worth stating that good agencies of course do want to satisfy their clients' demands, make successful placements and win repeat business. However it's worth noting that there are many who are simply after short-term profits with little thought to quality. Unfortunately the competitiveness of the marketplace has given rise to many sharp practices which are clearly at odds with the interests of both candidates and clients. From this point onwards it is assumed that you are going to manage your own recruitment activities and we will now run through the whole process step by step.

Get started by defining what you need – how to write an effective job specification

The single most important aspect of the hiring process is the planning stage and the preparation of a job specification is a key part of the planning process. Get this wrong and you are almost guaranteed not to succeed. Unclear expectations, vague reporting lines and ill defined responsibilities often lead to disappointment or many hours of wasted time and effort. This can often result in failing to find suitable candidates or actually hiring unsuitable candidates. A good job specification explains certain key points and should make sense to the person applying for the job, the hiring manager, colleagues or other staff with whom the person will be interacting and anybody involved in the recruitment process.

Key Points to be included in Job Specifications:

- A clear outline of the key duties and responsibilities and what the person will be doing. It can also be useful to illustrate the percentage of time allocated to each of the key tasks.

- An overview of the reporting relationships and where the person fits within the organisation.

- What outputs and deliverables the person is expected to produce.

- Make sure the job title is clear and will make sense to people from outside the company. Most people search for a job based on job titles, so if something is not easily understood it is very likely to get overlooked and you may miss out on suitable candidates who choose not to apply.

Beware that you can get carried away and end up throwing everything but the kitchen sink into a job specification. This can actually scare people off or confuse them. Generally when a candidate reads a job specification he or she needs to be able to form a clear view of what they will be doing on a daily basis and what they are expected to deliver. Try to keep focused on the performance requirements or key deliverables rather than getting fixated on minimum years of experience. High performers frequently have less experience than their peers. Indeed the definition of talent is the ability to do more with less or to deliver required results faster, cheaper or to a higher standard than peers. By specifying minimum years of experience you may indeed be ruling out highly capable and talented people. It is best to keep things simple – define what you need in terms of performance and key deliverables. Let potential candidates convince you that they are capable rather than just proving that they fit some generic template of previous experience and pre-defined skills.

> **Tip – when writing job specifications you should always:**
>
> - Avoid jargon
> - Use plain English
> - Use self-explanatory job titles

If you find yourself changing any of the key requirements in the job specification as you progress through the recruitment process then you probably haven't really adequately defined exactly what it is that you are after. If you don't really know what you need it's no surprise that it's difficult to find. Any decent recruiter will tell you that if they don't fully understand what's required they will have little chance of success. It's always useful to sense check what you think you need with the type of people you are trying to hire. This can be done by talking with existing employees, customers, suppliers, partners or anyone who's currently doing that type of work.

Remember that the job specification is not necessarily the job advert

Remember that the job specification will form the basis of the advert but it's not necessarily the full advert. We'll talk more about job adverts in Chapter 2. It's important to remember that the advert is written in a way so as to encourage the right type of person to apply for the role. Far too many people mix the two things up. Out of fear of breaching anti-discrimination laws they produce job specifications that are too vague or end up being bland to the point of being totally unappealing. You may well have to have certain jargon and information contained within an internal job specification document but keep it out of the advert. It's perfectly acceptable to use an advert to find suitable candidates and then once selected for interview to send candidates a more detailed job specification. Of course it's important not to fall foul of anti-discrimination legislation but there's no law stating that job adverts have to be boring.

Defining the person specification and assessing cultural fit

If, having discussed the requirements with all the interested parties, you have been able to write a clear job specification, it can be a very useful exercise to also define a person specification. The person specification is a useful tool in terms of identifying critical or beneficial skills and competencies that are required. Even more useful is the identification of the key attributes or capabilities of the person you want to hire. These are often endemic in the culture of your business and mean that people who possess these characteristics are much more likely to enjoy working for you as they are much more likely to achieve success for you. The person specification is a simple document that outlines the key attributes and capabilities. It will help you to focus on finding evidence of these factors during interviews. It is a good idea to involve the team in defining the key attributes and capabilities as they will have a clear understanding of what they are.

I strongly believe this is one of the most important aspects of developing a successful long-term talent acquisition and talent development strategy. Knowing the types of people that fit with your culture, understanding why they fit and why they stay, are vital ingredients to successful talent management, acquisition and retention.

Cultural fit is something we hear more and more about particularly from some of the world's largest companies. They often seem obsessed with the culture and values of their organisation and it's no wonder as it's an increasingly important issue. The reality is that company culture and the potential fit of any new hires is indeed very important. It is something you should definitely spend some time defining and understanding. Having a good appreciation of company culture is undoubtedly a very important part of the hiring process. Frequently the cause of poor hiring decisions can be traced back to a poor cultural fit for the person involved, and everybody concludes (invariably after the event of course) that he or she just didn't fit in. Firstly let's look at some basic definitions of what company culture is:

- It can be defined as the personality of a company.

- It can indicate the typical behaviours of people within a company and can include things like values, visions, norms, working language, beliefs and habits.

- It can be indicated by the type of environment that the company operates in.

Company culture can be seen in the way owners and employees think, feel and act. It can be seen in the types of behaviours that are encouraged, rewarded and celebrated and conversely in those that are shunned and discouraged. As companies grow in size owners or senior managers can't know every employee and can't be involved in every decision. A process or procedure cannot be created for every possible scenario or situation and so culture serves to give all employees a guiding framework to work within. Culture is normally the tone set by the senior leadership – their values and behaviours normally becomes the culture of the company as it grows.

Defining the culture of a company boils down to defining the types of behaviours and attitudes that are required or expected within the business. Sometimes this is not even consciously thought about or defined, but people will have a good feeling about what type of individual generally enjoys working within the company. Such individuals consequently fit well with the culture and perform well within the organisation. There are numerous examples of companies with very strong cultures, like the open entrepreneurial culture in the larger IT companies, or the more conservative and highly regulated culture within industries like financial services and banking.

It's very important to define the characteristics and typical behaviours of those who you deem to be successful and who add the most value within your company. Once identified and defined you can then go about making sure that these criteria are assessed during the hiring process. How do we do that? It's pretty straight forward really. We look for evidence that shows us the values and behaviours of potential candidates. It's here that I think many people struggle. How do I tell if somebody possesses entrepreneurial traits? You don't have to specifically tell them what you're looking for just ask some open-ended questions that require them to open up about themselves and how they work.

Tip – When trying to assess cultural fit make sure you ask very open questions that help to give you an insight into the typical behaviour and attitudes of a candidate. Examples would include:

- What's the ideal type of environment that you like to work in and why?
- What were the characteristics of the best manager you ever had and why did you enjoy working for him or her?

Be careful here, if somebody badly needs or wants your job then there's a temptation for them to lie or exaggerate in an effort to tell you what you want to hear. Be sure to challenge sweeping statements that claim all sorts of successes in solving problems. I find some good detailed exploratory questioning helps unearth the truth:

> **"That sounds great. Please tell me how you managed to achieve that?"**

> **"What barriers did you encounter along the way and how did you get around them?"**

> **"What did you personally do differently to what others have done in order to fix that issue?"**

> **"Please explain why you think you succeeded where others had failed?"**

Without actually having delivered tangible benefits people tend to struggle to give credible answers to such questions. Exaggeration of their own involvement or contribution is a very common technique for people looking to over-sell their experience or achievements. Their involvement may have been minimal but for the purpose of their CV or in an interview they want to claim all the credit. Very specific detailed questioning really helps to test the knowledge and ability of the candidate.

HIRE WITHOUT RECRUITMENT AGENCIES

This is an interviewing technique used by law enforcement agencies the world over when trying to trip somebody up with inconsistencies in their story. When asked for very detailed explanations of certain aspects of their story, people telling the truth are generally happy to explain any level of detail. Why wouldn't they, it's the truth. A red flag for deceptive behaviour is somebody who should know the details but doesn't and who becomes uncomfortable or agitated when pressed for specifics. There is further detailed discussion on interviewing techniques in Chapter 7.

I find it best to encourage and allow candidates to give an accurate and honest impression of who they are and how they like to work. The interview process should encourage this as much as possible. It's good practice to describe the culture of your company at the early stages of the process. You can allow people to self select themselves out of the process or out of applying altogether. If it's obvious that somebody won't fit with the culture, it's best for all concerned that the hiring process doesn't begin in the first place. Overall, in terms of assuring a good cultural fit, honesty is required on both sides of the table.

Ideally you will have been able to define a clear job specification and all involved are happy that it accurately reflects the expectations of the role. If you have also been able to develop a clear person specification for the person you want to hire then you have successfully passed the first hurdle. You are now ready to start looking for potential candidates.

CHAPTER 2: CANDIDATE SOURCING

In today's world, candidate sourcing has become a specialist discipline in its own right. The use of social media has exploded and it has become an essential tool in sourcing candidates. It is absolutely correct to separate the activities of candidate sourcing from candidate recruitment. To recruit a candidate means to interview and offer a person a job and for them to accept the role and become an employee. To source a candidate means to find and engage with a candidate with the aim of getting that candidate interested in discussing possible employment opportunities. It may seem pedantic to distinguish between the two but there are definite and specific differences that can make a material impact on how you hire people.

Candidate types

Candidates are characterised as being either active or passive. Active candidates, as the name implies are those who are actively looking for a new role. The reasons for them doing so are many and varied. Passive candidates are those who are not necessarily actively looking for a new role but if they have the right skills and experience they could possibly be a good fit for your business. Because of this potential interest to your business passive candidates are worth targeting in an effort to see if they will come and work for you. Take a look at Figure 1 which demonstrates the basic differences between active and passive candidates. Passive candidates will typically only be motivated by improved pay and conditions or improved prospects or even both. They're not actively looking for a new role so they need to be persuaded and tempted by the prospects of an improvement in their lot. Passive candidates can be further sub-divided into two categories:

Open Passive Candidates

This is the type of candidate who is open to ideas and may be persuaded to put themselves forward for a new role or opportunity. This type of candidate is often the top talent within a company, always looking to stretch and develop themselves. Frequently they will have spent between two and four years in a job and may well have a desire to move on to the next challenge. If they're not finding a suitable challenge within their current company then they may well consider opportunities outside of it. It's very important to make sure that your role is going to match their requirements in terms of what factors are important to them. You must take the time to understand their motivating factors. Your vacancy may present a great opportunity to develop new skills but if the salary is less than what they're getting now you are very unlikely to hire them. Of course this is not always the case as salary may not necessarily be the strongest motivating factor and it just might be outweighed by other factors. It is very important that you get an understanding of what their key motivating factors actually are.

Inactive Passive Candidates

Inactive candidates have generally been with the same company for a long time and are very comfortable and settled and extremely unlikely to move unless they are forced to. It's flattering for them to be contacted about potential new roles.

Most people will happily engage in some non-committal dialogue. The trick when dealing with inactive candidates is to make sure up front that what you have to offer is going to be appealing to them. It's best to clear this hurdle as early as possible before you waste a lot of time. Inactive passive candidates may only rarely be approached so remember they will be feeling flattered and will often display positive signals just out of mere curiosity even when they have no intention of leaving their current role.

Active versus Passive Candidates

Active Candidates
(Typically 25% of the Population)

Will be motivated by finding any type of suitable job

Open Passive Candidates
(Typically 60% of the Population)

Will be motivated by better pay and conditions, a career move, better prospects or any combination of these. They can become active candidates when approached with the right type of opportunity.

Inactive Passive Candidates
(Typically 15% of the Population)

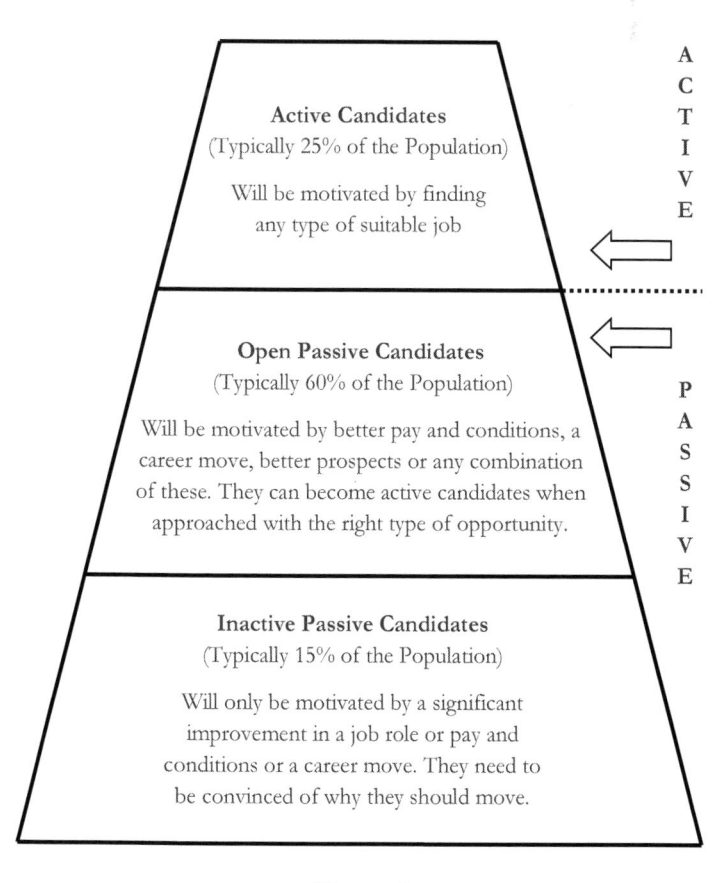

Will only be motivated by a significant improvement in a job role or pay and conditions or a career move. They need to be convinced of why they should move.

ACTIVE

PASSIVE

Figure 1

Initially we're going to look at sourcing active candidates. People frequently view active candidates in a negative way thinking that if they were any good they'd already have a job. This can be an unfair view, particularly during times of economic uncertainty when whole teams or divisions can be laid off or an entire company is closed down. It's absolutely right to ensure that you gain a full understanding of why a person is actively looking for a new role. It's vital to ensure that there's a plausible reason and you are perfectly entitled to ask what it is. Genuine candidates will have no issue with explaining the reasons why they are seeking a new role and what they are looking for. Any hesitation in this area is a red flag. It shows that the person may have something to hide if they are not prepared to go into detail and you should exercise caution in such circumstances. You do need to be convinced of the reasons but sometimes people can be embarrassed about the situation in which they find themselves due to personal circumstance so always be respectful and tread carefully.

At the start of the recruitment process it's advisable to immediately start looking for active candidates. They are willing participants, often available at reasonable notice. They are usually easier to hire than those who are targeted or "head-hunted". By starting to look for active candidates you are announcing your intentions to the market and creating an open competition for any interested applicants. Our intention is to ideally get a shortlist of three to five suitable candidates during the recruitment process. If we get less than this it leaves us with very little choice. If we get more than five candidates then we may end up wasting time doing excessive interviewing. You may not get enough suitable active candidates so you might have to try and directly source some passive candidates also. It does however make sense to immediately start advertising at the beginning of the process. A late entrant may come into the frame and if you are engaging with passive candidates the process will inevitably slow down, so it's good practice to have the advertising out there working on your behalf from the very start of the process.

Some businesses can be very effective at finding candidates, but often a lack of ability to source candidates means you don't even get the chance to start the recruitment process at all. Similarly a business may be excellent at sourcing interested candidates but will often fail to convert those applicants into employees. The aim of this chapter is to illustrate the myriad of candidate sourcing tools that may be available to you. In addition we will discuss the pros and cons of each. Finally we'll discuss how you can develop a winning strategy that works for you in getting what you need in the most effective way.

How to source active candidates

- Newspaper / magazine adverts

- Job boards / website adverts

- Your own company website

- Current / ex employee referrals

- Radio advertising

- Online CV databases

- Publicity / advertorials

- Online forums

- University / College career officers

- Twitter / Facebook / LinkedIn

- Blogs

- Career fairs

- Recruitment agencies

- Head hunters

- Professional bodies and trade associations

Table 1 shows the pros and cons of each sourcing method. Each one should be considered and ruled in or out depending on your own needs and budget. This list is of course by no means exhaustive but the aim of the exercise is to identify some of the commonly used methods and to make you think about any other options or methods that may help you to find suitable applicants. There is often a temptation to find some secret magic source of untapped candidates and articles are frequently written announcing the birth of some new miracle candidate sourcing method that will leave all others in its wake. The reality is that effective candidate sourcing requires a broad brush approach. You need to regularly assess how you're doing and what new areas you can be explore. It's a dynamic and ever changing aspect of hiring the right people.

Sourcing Method	Pros	Cons
Newspaper & Magazine Adverts	Helps to build profile of your brand or business.	Expensive. Often ineffective.
Job Boards & Websites	Cost Effective. Wide Reach. Adaptable.	Can attract less than high quality applications. Can attract very high volumes of applications.
Your own company Website	It's free for you to use. You're in control.	It may not have the widest audience.
Current & Ex Employee Referrals	Referrals are often a good fit. They will have a good understanding of the culture and will already know quite a bit about your business.	Overuse in hiring referred candidates can encourage the same type of person being repeatedly hired.
Radio Advertising	Reaches a wide audience. Good brand building.	Can be expensive.

Table 1

Sourcing Method	Pros	Cons
Online CV databases	Cost effective.	Some of the CVs may be quite old and may have turned into passive candidates by the time you've found their CVs.
Publicity / Advertorials	Often free. Best used in conjunction with other methods.	You need to write the materials yourself.
Online Forums	Directly marketing to industry or discipline specialists.	Can be difficult to access this type of channel. They require significant effort to engage effectively within these forums.
University / College Career Officers	Can be very effective. No associated cost.	Can be competitive with companies fighting over the best candidates.
Twitter / Facebook / LinkedIn	Becoming increasingly popular. Effective if used in the right way. Twitter and Facebook have little or no associated costs.	Can take significant time commitments to build up a following and requires commitment to become an active participant.

Table 1 continued

Sourcing Method	Pros	Cons
Blogs	Often have very specific audiences.	Can take significant time commitments to identify suitable blogs or to build up a following of your own.
Career Fairs	Can have a very specific audience of active or open passive candidates.	Variable costs. Can involve significant preparation time and effort.
Recruitment Agencies	Can provide a quick response. Can be reasonably good if they know your business/culture. Can sometimes give you access to exclusive candidates.	Expensive and often deliver little value for money. If you use more than one at a time it can create image problems for you or give mixed messages to the marketplace.
Head hunters	Can give you access to exclusive candidates. Can provide market knowledge on salaries and other market information.	Expensive.
Professional Bodies & Trade Associations	Can give direct access to professional candidates.	Some can be expensive.

Table 1 continued

How do candidate sourcing methods work?

Newspaper / Magazine Adverts

You pay for an advert in the magazine or newspaper – they have sliding scales of price depending upon size, etc. Most have salespeople who will happily quote large readership and distribution numbers to you. Ask them to give you an example of an advert that worked well for a business like yours. If they can't, then why consider this as an option at all? For the significant costs involved I would be seeking strong assurances that your money is going to yield a positive result. Most papers / magazines have a website and your ad gets posted there also. These types of advertising media are certainly becoming less and less effective and it's not unusual to waste every single penny you spend on them.

Job Boards / Website Adverts

You pay for an advert slot, and typically these last for two to four weeks. These vary in price and indeed some are free. You may have to run several on a trial-and-error basis but this is one of the most cost effective means of hiring people today. A well designed job advert can be very effective indeed. We'll discuss this point in further detail later in this chapter.

Your own company website

You create your own careers page or links to other job advertising sites where you have vacancies advertised and candidates apply directly to your adverts.

Current / Ex Employee referrals

Tell everybody in your business that you're hiring and what you're looking for. Lots of companies offer financial incentives to employees when one of their referred candidates is hired. Rewards can range from £100 to over £2,000 for very specialist roles.

Radio Advertising

You pay for individual or batches of advertising slots. Most stations will also provide facilities to produce the advert.

Online CV databases

Most job boards now also have databases where candidates post their CVs in the hope of being contacted directly by recruiters. Generally you pay to have access. Either you pay for the CVs you download or you pay for access for a fixed period of time. All have systems in place to prevent abuse; for example, they will have reasonable download limits to prevent the downloading of thousands of CVs.

Publicity / Advertorials

This is a great way to spread the word and let everybody know that you're hiring. With so many media platforms out there, editors are always crying out for content. If you can spin your hiring need into a good story, you're sure to find somebody out there happy to publish it in a local paper or trade magazine.

Online Forums

There is a myriad of online forums to support discussions on a vast range of topics. These can be run by individuals or indeed professional bodies. You can find them by searching online yourself or by talking to peers and asking them to recommend suitable options for you. You can join up directly and post updates about your hiring needs. Some have direct advertising sections for job vacancies or others will do it for you if you contact the administrator of the site. Some charge a fee but they tend to be very reasonable. You may have to experiment with a few before you find those that meet your needs. The good thing is that once you know it works, you can keep coming back to it.

University / College Career Officers

This is an excellent source of candidates. Universities and colleges are always very keen to see their graduates move onto jobs and those involved in the careers section are usually very helpful and proactive people. It's worth bearing in mind that these routes are not just for recent graduates. Most have active alumni that you can reach through the careers office. It's also worth bearing in mind that very often post-graduate students already have experience and may be looking to get back to work again after graduation.

Twitter / Facebook / LinkedIn

All three can be good routes to finding suitable candidates. You will find large numbers of people praising and criticising these tools in equal measure with regard to their suitability for hiring people. In very basic terms I would categorise LinkedIn as a networking tool for professionals. Most people on there will be passive candidates and they are on there to showcase their experience and abilities in the hope of being found for a job which is significantly better than what they currently have. You can search for people and contact them to see if they're interested in your role. You can also set up a company page that people can follow and you can post updates to allow people to apply for your jobs. It can be useful for keeping your talent pool of interested candidates updated with what's happening within your business

Twitter can be good for time-bound large scale recruitment drives, such as graduate programmes, large events, etc. It lends itself to activities that require multiple updates on an hourly or daily basis and can keep people in touch with the very latest status.

Facebook, in my opinion, is good for the promotion of small local businesses. Posts can be created and shared by employees amongst their contacts and customers can follow the page for updates about the business. I would be dubious about the value of using Facebook for professional services or larger types of business. It can be a useful resource if your target audience are frequent users and so can also be used to let people know that you are hiring.

Blogs

Good blogs tend to have a lot of followers, regular updates as well as discussions. You may find blogs which have followers who are exactly the type of person you're trying to find. Care is needed as it is poor form to try and hijack someone else's blog for your own selfish purposes. I would recommend contacting the owner and seeking permission to post messages about vacancies. The other option of course is to set up your own blog and build up a suitable following of possible future candidates to hire. This can be very successful but bear in mind blogs require a lot of effort and must be updated regularly with interesting content otherwise people will just stop following them.

Career Fairs

They can be an excellent source of candidates and can be a very good way to get honest market feedback from possible suitable candidates. You'll get a chance to chat with real live job seekers and you can use the time to increase your understanding of their motivations. You may even come across a suitable person to hire. Do bear in mind that costs vary and the results from such events can vary widely.

Recruitment Agencies

As per previous discussions agencies are really only of use to you if they have the ability to understand your business and give you access to candidates that you can't otherwise engage with.

Head Hunters

These really should only be used for high-end senior positions where no suitable candidates are available in the open market or absolute discretion and confidentiality is required because of the business situation.

Professional Bodies / Trade Associations

These are often a very good direct route to professionally qualified and experienced candidates. Costs can vary from free to very expensive depending upon individual groups. They will often have excellent networking events and facilities.

How to write a good Job Advert

You need to make sure that your job advert highlights the attributes and characteristics of the person you're trying to hire. You also need to highlight why these attributes and characteristics are required. Go onto any job board and you'll see a wide range in standards of job adverts. Some will have been written in a lazy and sloppy manner and would only appeal to somebody who really is desperate for a job. Take a look on the main job boards such as Totaljobs, Monster, Jobsite or Indeed and you'll see a wide variety in quality.

The basic rules of marketing apply just as much to job advertising just as they apply to any type of advertising. You must have content that attracts the attention of potential candidates. Often this simply means having the right job title. Too often you see titles which are vague or full of company terminology that won't make sense to external candidates. You may call your receptionist a "customer facing service operative" but when you're competing with hundreds or even thousands of other adverts out there you need a title that people will quickly understand and identify with. People will search for jobs by job title. A title such as "estate agency lettings administrator" is quickly and easily understood. A title such as "technical infrastructure manager" could mean any number of different things and could apply to many widely differing industries. It's far too vague and may well be ignored.

A quick look on any of the CV databases will often show you the common job titles that people are using. Make sure to consider alternative titles that mean the same thing to different people. What some companies call business development managers are called account managers, territory managers or relationship managers in others. By role playing as an actual candidate and spending some time online you can find the typical titles that you'll be competing against. Ask some people currently doing the job what keywords they would use if they were looking for a job.

Now that you've caught the person's attention with an appropriate job title you need to generate some interest with your content. Here you need to explain what the company does and how it does it. If the reason for hiring is a good selling point then make sure to use it to sell the job. For example internal progression is great attractor for people. Statements like:

> "Due to an internal promotion we are currently looking for a new ...."

can really entice motivated and enthusiastic people looking to progress within an organisation. Growth is another great motivator, as is winning new contracts or customers etc.

It's also very important to give an overview of what the company is like to work for. If yours is a very dynamic and demanding environment with little or no bureaucracy and no appetite for bureaucrats you might say something like:

> "Ours is a challenging and dynamic business not bound by unnecessary constraints. Our culture is one where risk taking and entrepreneurial spirit is encouraged and rewarded."

This will actually serve to put certain people off the role and that's what you want to achieve, allow those unsuitable types of candidates to self-select themselves as being unsuitable for the position. It really is a case of horses for courses – there's little point wasting time interviewing people who are never going to fit in with your company culture. It goes the other way as well of course – we all want reliable, conservative and prudent people managing our pension funds and if you're hiring for that kind of person you should tell people that's what you need; the swashbuckling and creative, entrepreneurial types will steer well clear of this type of role.

> Tip – you should always give candidates an opportunity to "self-select" themselves. This is achieved by giving them a clear explanation of the type of person that you're looking for. If having read your advert they conclude they are not suitable then it saves wasted time for everybody.

If you've kept their interest so far, you now need to entice the suitable candidate to apply for the job. This is where you need to think about what's in it for the applicant. If the role is highly technically challenging; that can be rewarding in it-self. Lots of people get a kick out of solving difficult problems. Don't overdo it in the advert though; keep it to the main responsibilities – ideally four to seven bullet points. For any suitable candidates that you are going to meet you can always provide a more detailed specification after they've applied. The main point here is that when people are job hunting they want to form a general opinion as to whether the job and the business are of interest or not. Because of the very crowded job advertising market the time is not really there to spend half an hour reading an overly detailed advert. Make sure to use appropriate language that the type of person you're trying to appeal to would use. Again find somebody doing the job already and ask for their opinion on your advert and its content.

People frequently say that Internet advertising is a waste of time, that it only attracts unsuitable and poor candidates. I strongly disagree with that and I have to say that poorly worded job adverts have a lot to do with it. Poorly worded, vague and lazy job adverts posted on the Internet certainly are a waste of time but that's not the fault of the Internet. Failing to really specify what's required and the use of vague language does nothing to help applicants decide whether they're suitable or not. A decision has to be taken by the reader – does this company sound of interest to me and if yes is there a possibility that they may have an interest in me as a candidate. If your advert does not allow them to make such a decision then they may well apply anyway – nothing ventured, nothing gained.

Why are keywords so important in job adverts?

Remember we now live in a Search Engine Optimisation world. Businesses live and die by virtue of how easy they are to find with an internet search. The same principles apply to job advertising. Make sure to include any relevant keywords to aid your search rankings. Think about the top three to four skills that are required in the role and make sure to include them in your advert. I'm talking about the kinds of keywords that people are going to be searching for. Examples would be specific software tools or specific accounting packages. Remember to do a search on other adverts in your relevant market place. If you find other companies using different terms you may well want to include these terms into your job advert to ensure that they show up in searches. What one company calls an accounts receivables officer can also be known as an:

- Accounts receivable analyst

- Accounts receivable associate

- Accounts receivable specialist

- Accounts receivable executive

- Accounts receivable administrator

- Accounts receivable assistant

- Accounts receivable clerk

- Accounting assistant

- Accounts administrator

- Assistant accountant

- Credit controller

- Accounting analyst

Tip – advert format guidelines:

- Keep sentences as brief as possible - bullet points are good. 15-20 words per sentence helps with making things read well.

- Avoid Capital Letter, Italics and abbreviations or if you must use them please put the full wording in brackets so it is crystal clear to the reader what the meaning is.

- Use plain simple fonts such as Arial, Tahoma or Times New Roman.

Thinking about it from a job hunter's perspective you need to make sure that your advert will be found. You need to include any relevant keywords to make sure that they show up in searches. All search engines basically work off a word count basis – they prioritise certain things like the job title and then simply count the number of times the keyword appears in the advert. Often job advertising websites allow you to add specific additional keywords (known as Tags) that don't necessarily get shown in the main advert text but do help in making sure that your advert is found when job hunters are entering search terms. Jobs in any search are listed in order of ranking as defined by the title and number of keywords contained in the text and Tags of the advert. You certainly don't need to be an expert to make sure your adverts are written in a way that ensures they will be highly ranked in search results. The basic principles are pretty simple but you do need to be aware of how the ranking systems work as there's little point in having an advert that won't be found. Take a look at some of the major job boards as they all have simple guides that will show you how to optimise your adverts.

How to develop your candidate sourcing strategy

Now is the point where you need to try to get inside the mind of the type of person that you're hoping will be interested in working for you. This can be easier said than done. You need to find and engage with somebody who is a member of your target market and who's happy to have an open conversation with you. You need to find out where they look for jobs and what particular types of media they use. For example these days very few people read the newspaper in the expectation of finding a job and indeed amongst certain age brackets newspaper reading is very low. Amongst that particular group, social media activity may be very high so that's where you would be looking to engage with such people. It also depends on how specialised the people are that you're trying to hire. What you need is advice from somebody from the target market about where they would typically look for work, or if they have a rare or specialist skill set you need to find out how other businesses approach them about possible opportunities. Again this is a subtle but important difference. In times of busy market places and skills shortages advertising may be wasted as everybody with the skills you're after is already in work (well the competent ones anyway). They will not be looking at job adverts, or they may be ignoring them even when they're right in front of them.

The key thing is to find ways of accessing the right potential target market. Once you have found a way to reach even a small number of such people then you need to explore this in greater detail and make sure to maximise that channel. It really is invaluable to have a direct conversation with such people. I mean a real quality conversation. I have frequently contacted people that I don't know in order to ask their advice. I'll start a conversation with something like:

> **"I'm recruiting for XYZ at the moment, you look like somebody they'd really need to try and get into their business, but I'm not sure that the current openings would offer enough challenge to a person of your experience".**

This tends to open up a double-sided conversation – we get to discuss the role and the company but also what the other person is looking for and what they'd seek in a role. These can be very useful discussions and will help to understand why your job doesn't appeal to them (even though they could certainly do it). Armed with this kind of insight you can take corrective action either in your package, or advertising or responsibilities, etc. Most agency recruiters will not go to this level of detail; they simply don't have the time unless you have paid them an up-front fee.

I have hired a lot of people through this kind of dialogue. They really appreciate the fact that you're not trying to force them into a role. Often they can recommend somebody suitable or where you might find people who may be interested. They will also be happy to return your call when you leave a message six months later saying you now have a role that fits their requirements. This is mainly because you've taken the time to listen to what they want. Never underestimate the value of having quality conversations with good people. I would always target higher quality candidates for this type of exercise, the ones who have shown a consistent trend of achievement and delivery on their CV, as well steady career progression. They are generally the more level-headed and less arrogant types of people with whom you can really engage. Often I have found that the more spectacular CVs tend to belong to egomaniacs who can be hard to deal with. Such people in my experience often harbour insecurities or inadequacies which cause them to behave in an exaggerated fashion and you rarely learn anything from talking to them, other than how great they are, of course.

At this point you really need to pay attention to the source of those interesting candidates. If you find a suitable CV and they happen to have a specific qualification, now is the time to do some more detailed searches for people who may have the same or similar qualifications. As mentioned earlier, most educational establishments are extremely helpful if you're looking for people to hire. Make sure to contact any relevant institutions and let them know what you're looking for.

Now you also need to think about getting the message out in terms advertising. Here your best tactic is a bit of role reversal. Act like you are the candidate and you're looking for a job. Go online and try to find a suitable job opening. Spend two to three hours doing this and I guarantee you'll find some interesting results. What you're looking for here are the job boards that have similar roles. You'll also find specialist websites and forums that have job advertising sections such as trade associations, university and professional body websites for example. Most of these tend be very cost effective; a lot are free. If you find that some of the specific websites are expensive, ask for a free trial. Many will only sell you a one year subscription. Be wary of this unless you can justify the cost. I have found that many of the higher quality websites will provide you with a free trial advert or a free search activity that lasts for a day or two. They are happy to do this as they are confident that you'll be impressed with the results you'll get. It's worth bearing in mind that these websites are constantly evolving due to the transient nature of the job hunting market. What is a perfect fit for your business today could be less than optimal in twelve month's time. I'd recommend that you evaluate your sourcing methods every six months or so. Make sure that you make note of the basic metrics of applications per job and percentage of relevant applications.

The initial aim in terms of candidate sourcing is to begin to build a pipeline of potentially suitable candidates. Once that pipeline begins to flow it's time to focus on the quality and suitability and to sharpen your focus onto those strategies that are going to yield the most suitable candidates for you.

CHAPTER 3: HOW TO FIND PASSIVE CANDIDATES

Can't find suitable CVs?

It's not unusual to receive high volumes of wholly unsuitable CVs in response to job adverts. It's very frustrating and can be very time consuming having to review large numbers of CVs. Most of the techniques we've mentioned to date have been aimed at sourcing active candidates. Ideally this is the way to go if there are suitable people available who are prepared to apply for a job that you have advertised. If you can't find enough or indeed any suitable applicants at all then you need to try and identify and track down some passive candidates. You're going after those who aren't necessarily looking for a new role but who possess the skills and abilities that you need.

Your ultimate aim in sourcing passive candidates is to get suitable people to engage with you. You're not necessarily getting them to actually apply for a job, well not initially anyway. You merely want to engage them in open dialogue and bring them around to thinking about the possibility of working for you. A lot of people do not want to be seen to be openly applying for positions, particularly if it's with a competitor, a customer or a supplier. Contacting people in a "cold – calling" manner is a very different ballgame to sourcing active candidates. People very often mistakenly think the approach to communicating with a passive candidate is the same as that for an active candidate. It's not.

In order to engage effectively with passive candidates, contact needs to be made by somebody with a good knowledge of the business, who can have a high quality conversation. They need to be able to convince the target person that it's worth their while. It also needs to be approached with a degree of patience and you need to give the candidate time to think and to do some research to decide that yours is a company worth working for. You need to identify somebody with decent communication skills to carry out such tasks. Having a patient outlook on life also helps, as most approaches don't end in success. If done properly then each conversation will yield some useful information, a possible candidate for the future or maybe a referral of somebody else that the person knows who might be suitable and possibly interested in your vacancy. Competent professional recruiters generally possess these traits. They will be well used to chasing down a hundred possible leads in the hope of finding one suitable and interested candidate. For now let's look at the ways of sourcing candidates and the main differences between active and passive candidates.

Passive Candidate Sourcing Techniques

- Current and ex - employees (making referrals)

- Social Media (Facebook, LinkedIn, Twitter, YouTube)

- Universities / schools / colleges (current or previous students who may be looking for work)

- Conferences (networking)

- Customers (referrals)

- Suppliers (referrals)

- Online Boolean searches (to identify possible suitable target candidates)

- Reference checks (can often make further referrals)

How to get candidate referrals

Networking and associated candidate referrals have become a major candidate sourcing method. The main point of these activities is to identify some potential candidates which we are confident will be a good fit for our business and our current role. Chapter 6 will expand on the topic of how to spread the message that you're hiring but for now the key principle is that we must get the message out. Everybody who knows your business and who may know potential candidates must be aware that you're hiring and must know exactly how to recommend somebody. If somebody is considering looking for a new job they will frequently have discussed the situation with friends, family, colleagues, relatives and contacts in general. Before they actively start looking for work their contacts may well be aware that they are open to ideas. This is a perfect time to be approaching a passive candidate, as they are about to become active. You are getting in touch with them before they are talking to anybody else.

Basics of Boolean Searching

The use of Boolean searching is widespread in the recruitment industry. By using such techniques we are trying to identify people by virtue of their job title or current employer. Once we have identified suitable people we are approaching them to see if they might be interested in discussing possible opportunities with our company or if they could recommend somebody suitable to us. Unlike referrals, we don't know these people at all so it can be a risky process. We are assuming competence and a degree of suitability because of the current position that they hold and because they are working for a company whose business is similar to our own. It is similar in terms of risk, to hiring active candidates.

Increasing numbers of people are posting their CVs online in the hope that recruiters will find them and offer them work. It is also becoming much easier to find possible candidates by searching online for job titles and company names. Having identified a person's name and employer, their contact details are generally pretty straightforward to find. A quick search online will yield numerous website articles on how to find email addresses for people. If you're not comfortable doing this type of thing there are plenty of research companies out there who can help you or indeed you could engage the help of a freelance recruiter.

Once we have the contact details of the target person we can then make a direct approach to them. Most sourcing companies will generally just look for a company name and a job title and will then make direct contact with people to see if they're open to ideas. It really is nothing more sophisticated than that. Such headhunting activities are really just fishing exercises to try and find suitable candidates. There's nothing stopping you from conducting similar exercises, assuming that you have the time and resources to do so. Searching for job titles and company names will often show up results in a wide range of published materials, some examples, that show how wide ranging these can be, are:

- Conference attendance lists

- Published articles or reports

- Testimonials for service providers such as training companies

- Online profiles and CVs

- Directories and membership lists of professional bodies and associations

- Press releases or media stories

- Online professional discussion forums

- YouTube videos of professional accomplishments and achievements, or product promotional videos

- Customer recommendations

If you feel shy in any way about approaching people, there are many simple flattery techniques that can be used to approach people. Saying something like:

> **"I read your recent article on "xyz". Our company is currently looking to find an experienced X and I felt somebody with your obvious industry expertise and knowledge may possibly know someone who might be interested in our vacancy."**

This leaves the door open for them to recommend themselves if they are so inclined or indeed to make a referral. In my experience as long as people understand why it is that you're approaching them and you are giving a clear and concise explanation of what you're looking for, most people are generally open enough to helping out by mentioning a name or two. Searching for inactive candidates is becoming an increasingly specialised area and there are many free articles online giving tips on how to carry out detailed Boolean forensic searches. Training courses are now common and are often aimed at the novice. You can spend a day on such a course and become quite knowledgeable in this area. You can of course also engage a professional search consultant or a freelance recruiter to help you.

The thing to bear in mind about passive candidate engagement is that it's very useful in terms of getting market feedback, and learning what does and does not appeal to potential candidates about your business and the role(s) you're looking to fill. It can however turn out to be a frustrating experience if you just need to fill jobs in the short term. The success rate can be very low. In my experience, engagement with passive candidates can and does yield results but, unless you're offering a fantastic position or really good salaries, the odds of tempting somebody out of an existing job to take your offer are quite low.

Figure 2 shows that all types of passive candidates are typically of a higher quality, in the sense that we are approaching them directly because we know they have the experience and/or qualities that we're after. Active candidates directly applying for a new role are generally doing so for a direct, immediate reason. In that sense they are highly motivated to try to convince you that they are a suitable person and often may have convinced themselves even if they are less than ideal for the role in reality. The main motivating factor for active candidates is fear – fear of losing their current job; fear of actually having no job; fear of having no income in the long term; fear of where their current job is going, fear that their current boss does not have their best interests at heart.

HIRE WITHOUT RECRUITMENT AGENCIES

Active Candidates **Passive Candidates**

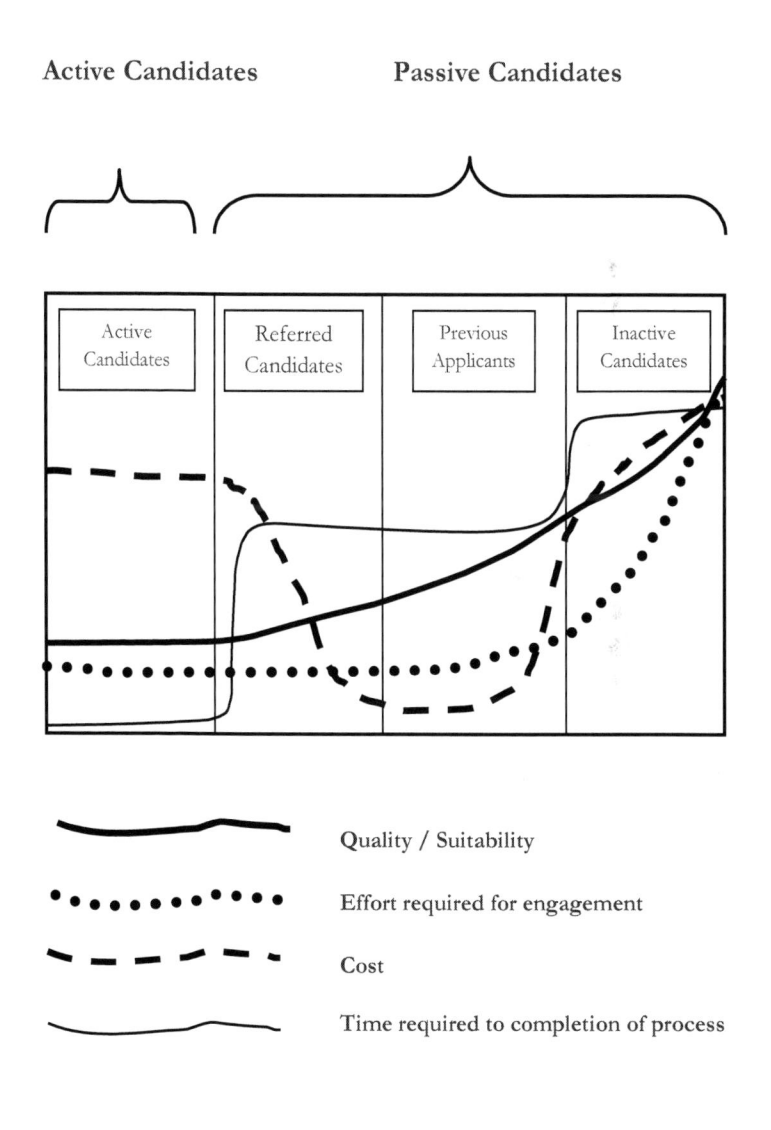

	Quality / Suitability
	Effort required for engagement
	Cost
	Time required to completion of process

Figure 2

Inactive candidates will be typically motivated by greed. Approaches to inactive candidates very often facilitate ego stroking and you can potentially waste a lot of time and effort for no result. Everybody's happy to hear that they've been recommended or headhunted and will naturally be curious to listen to what might be on offer. Inactive candidates will typically be happy in their current role, will be resistant to change and will be very likely to accept a counter-offer from their current employer if you do end up offering them a job.

In terms of speed and your level of control in the hiring and negotiation process, active candidates are far easier to deal with. They need a job and are inclined to accede to your requirements when negotiating. If you cannot source suitable active candidates then you must proceed to the sourcing of passive candidates. Indeed it's often a good idea if you have access to both types of candidate to include them in the recruitment process. The best situation to be in is to have two or more potentially suitable candidates. It really strengthens your negotiating stance to know you have a second option to fall back on if things are not going well with one particular candidate.

Passive candidates by their very nature are entering the process thinking they have nothing to prove. You need them far more than they need you. They are motivated by greed and as such can be awkward animals to negotiate with – indeed the process can often become protracted and, if they do get as far as resigning, counter-offers can then delay or destroy the process for you. Bear in mind also that by engaging them in the hiring process you may have converted them into active candidates and that they may now be also talking to other prospective employers. This often happens when people get the impression that their skills and experience are highly sought after in the general market place.

In conclusion, identifying potential targets can be done relatively easily if you approach it correctly, but it does take time and perseverance. It's always best if you can deal with active applicants for the variety of reasons already outlined. Every now and then you may have to approach inactive candidates, so it's useful knowledge to have. If done properly it can really teach you a lot about the job market you're operating in.

Widening your talent sourcing focus

Not being able to source suitable candidates is a frequent problem for many businesses. It's certainly not unusual to find it difficult to source people whose experience is directly relevant to your vacancy. I find this really is a mindset issue. Good talented people are generally very adaptable and it's quite common to hear of stories where people have successfully transferred into new industries. This is becoming increasingly common particularly when you consider that the average time spent in a role is something like three to four years.

Going back to your person specification, if you can find the right type of person who has the right characteristics that will allow them to fit with your company culture, then you have a good starting point. If you are convinced of the person's willingness and ability to learn, I would always put a higher value on ability and attitude than relevant experience alone.

When discussing sourcing difficulties with hiring managers I always ask if all the existing employees had directly relevant experience when they were hired. The answer is invariably no, we got lucky with some individuals who managed to learn how our business works and fitted in quickly. Upon further investigation it's always clear that luck has very little to do with it. If you're open-minded to hiring somebody who doesn't have relevant experience but who does exhibit the desired characteristics and attitudes then they have a very good chance of working out well for the business. I'm not aware of any such studies, but anecdotally I'm pretty sure there's actually very little correlation between relevance of prior experience and staff performance once they're in the job. I find it odd then that this is often the main criteria that hiring managers use when evaluating CVs.

It should also be borne in mind that many sectors have much more in common than people realise. For example, being able to use one Computer Aided Drawing, payroll or project planning software package means you stand a pretty good chance of being able to learn a new package pretty quickly. How many times have you seen hiring managers wait several months to find the perfect person when they could have hired somebody who could have been fully trained up within three to four weeks?

If you're not sure about the transferability of certain skills or experience, then talk to an applicant and ask them to convince you of how they would ensure an effective transfer into your business. If you're prepared to listen and consider what they're saying, this will give you some useful points to consider. Very often you'll have your mind changed.

Networking amongst customers, suppliers and competitors can also give you some hints as to what others are doing to get over their skills shortages. Don't forget to talk to existing employees too. Their insights can be invaluable in highlighting how they managed to learn the key things needed to get on within the business. I find that very often there may be two or three key things required to be successful in a role and these are often not necessarily related to experience at all. In other words, the ability to successfully do a job is not necessarily solely down to having a minimum amount of experience. Talented people often don't need experience. They rely on ability and sound judgement to deliver results. The very definition of talent is the ability to do things that others can't do or to do things using fewer resources or less time than others might need to achieve the same result.

Look for evidence or even potential evidence of these key characteristics when reviewing CVs or interviewing candidates. I have found you can tell a lot about a person by the language they use. How they phrase things in the written or spoken word often tells us a lot about their view of the world and how they approach every-day situations. People who tend to deliver good results and see things through to completion without getting distracted or deflected will have CVs that highlight very tangible, specific details showing the exact results. People that tend to refer to wide ranging responsibilities claiming to have delivered huge expansive improvements and projects frequently don't have a good eye for detail, but may have strengths in seeing the bigger picture. Such people are often strong in managing large projects and delegating tasks without getting into details.

At best, a CV is a mere snapshot of how the person is trying to sell themselves. The job of the interviewer is to use the CV as a guide to gain a more in-depth understanding of the characteristics, typical behaviours, strengths, weaknesses, capabilities and potential of the candidate. At worst the CV may be a complete fabrication or misrepresentation in order to fool you into giving the person a job that they desperately need. It does however serve as a very good guide to exploring what the person is trying to sell about themselves. Sometimes it can be greatly exaggerated; or indeed it can be understated. This will come out in the interview, where you will be convinced either way if the person has the characteristics you're after. My advice for interviews is that you should try to find out what the person is really like and how they actually go about doing the job. The aim is to get a fair and accurate indication of the person's working style, without making a final judgement until after the interview has been completed. There will be more on this important point in Chapter 7 Interviewing: getting the most out of the process.

CHAPTER 4: DEVELOPING A TALENT POOL

We concluded in Chapter 3 (How to find passive candidates) that sourcing passive candidates for our current open positions will be quite an unlikely route to success. One of the main reasons for this is that passive candidates can only be turned into active candidates if their key motivating factors are met. If our current job opening does not satisfy our passive candidate's desires then we will fail to convert them into an active candidate. Next we're going to look at developing a talent pool and how to proactively develop a pipeline of potentially suitable future candidates. This is a much more long term and strategic type approach to making sure our future vacancies will be filled in a timely manner as and when they arise.

Where the sourcing of passive candidates does work is usually for future vacancies that will meet the requirements of what the candidate is looking for in a role. In other words we have found a candidate that will fit with our company culture. We have also confirmed that they are interested in working for us. We don't have a suitable vacancy at the moment, but we probably will do in the future. It's really the opposite of active candidate sourcing – we source the future employee in advance of having the vacancy.

By way of example let's assume you engage with a potential hire. You discuss what they want to do, how their experience fits the business etc. If your current job opening doesn't fit their requirements for whatever reason you explore the reasons why not. You also explore what would fit with their requirements. You then agree to stay in touch. At some time in the future a job opening does come up which would be a strong fit for their skills and ability. At that point you go back to them and now they're the perfect candidate – see what I'm driving at here. Trying to push candidates into a job can be a fruitless exercise. Understanding people, their strengths, characteristics and abilities and then matching those to a suitable opportunity when it comes along – that's talent acquisition.

The timing, salary, situation, career potential etc. may not be 100% right and that may prevent someone from taking up a job opening with you right now. This can be a frustrating result but it's very important to not let it put a dampener on things. Closing out the situation where everybody feels good and the door is left open is always a good idea. Now I'm not saying that you shouldn't reject people if they're not a suitable fit. If they are not likely to fit with your business needs then it's important for you to be honest with people and let them know that you won't be progressing with them. What I am saying is that if you have identified a talented individual who you are confident would be a very good fit for your business then you shouldn't waste the opportunity to keep in touch with that person. You need to put them into your talent pool of potential future employees. Very often it can be one specific issue that stops someone taking a role and over the course of time that can change. Today's rejected job offer can turn into a very easy future hire if you go to the trouble to fully understand why the person is unable to come and work for you right now. Time spent doing this ensures you will know when the right opportunity comes along and you will find it easy to convince them that it is the right opportunity as you will know that it meets their expectations.

Converting "Applicants" into "Apployees"

This type of candidate I would label as an "Apployee". They start out as an applicant or we turn them into an applicant by engaging them in a discussion about potential employment opportunities. Throughout the process we turn them into an employee, but only once we've actually hired them. It's a process involving many steps and what we're doing when developing a talent pool is getting most of the hiring steps out of the way in advance of actually having a suitable job opening for the person. We do this so that when a suitable job does come along the final stages of actually hiring the person can be done quickly and efficiently. Both sides already know enough about each other that it's simply a case of completing the final contractual steps and the person's hired. This can work at all levels from graduate recruitment up to senior levels.

This type of situation would be a good example of the "unadvertised" job market you so often hear about. Before the job even gets to an advert format you already have the perfect candidate in mind. The conversational tone used when souring candidates for your talent pool is very different to that used with direct applications from "active" candidates. You have to be seen to be much more considerate of the person's desires and motivations and not just focused on our own immediate pressing requirements:

Passive candidate / applicant =

> "Let me tell you about this job I have and let's see if you're suitable and interested."

"Apployee" =

> "Remember when we discussed the kind of challenge that would interest you and you highlighted that you're looking for xyz. Well I have just such an opportunity. Let me tell you why it's the perfect job for you."

This is where good recruiters earn their money and genuinely add value for the clients and candidates they work with. Being able to manage and co-ordinate discussions of this type is the essence of a talent acquisition strategy. It's a very different to the approach taken when the sole aim is to fill an open vacancy as quickly as possible. When filling an open vacancy the priority is finding and short-listing suitable, interested and available candidates and getting the shortlist together in order to commence an effective interview and offer process.

Engage a professional recruiter to help you

As mentioned earlier a professional recruiter will be skilled at having good open conversations with people to identify their key expectations in considering possible new roles. Engaging a recruiter to work directly for you can be good idea if you're looking at proactive sourcing or developing a long term talent acquisition strategy. You may be able to get access to a dedicated recruiter through a suitable agency or indeed many good recruiters work on a freelance basis and you can effectively buy some of their time.

You need to be sure that you've found a recruiter who will properly represent your business and that you will be happy to have them approaching people on your behalf.

How do you know when you meet a good recruiter?

- They'll ask you lots of questions about the role and your business and why you're looking to hire.

- They may question you to the point of annoyance but they will be able to explain why their questions are relevant.

- They'll know their own performance ratios in terms of hires made / interviews conducted, interviews / offers issued, offers made / offers accepted. They will be able to explain what these ratios should be.

- Ask them what's the best placement they ever made and why. Get them to explain to you specifically what they did to make it happen. If you're impressed by what you hear then you know you've found somebody who can help you.

Pay them a salary with a small delivery bonus – don't over incentivise the hiring process, it makes people edgy and prone to delivering fast results to get the quick buck, rather than doing it properly.

Nominate your talent sourcing champion

If you're unable to get access to a professional recruiter then you do need to nominate somebody in your organisation who will take on the role of talent sourcing champion. This should be somebody who is knowledgeable and enthusiastic about the business. They must be a strong and confident communicator with good organisational skills. They definitely must not be shy about approaching people and they need to be flexible and adaptable. Situations may arise where a degree of risk taking is required. Fortune definitely favours the brave where candidate sourcing is concerned. Shrinking violets tend not to excel in the area of talent sourcing. It's often assumed that a HR professional is the best person to do this role, often that's not the case. Make sure to identify the person in your team that is going to be able sell the business most effectively. They must be capable of opportunistically finding, chasing down and impressing potential high calibre new hires. As long as your talent champion possesses this ability then you're on the right track.

CHAPTER 5: HOW TO READ AND SHORTLIST CVS

This seems to be an area that really annoys a lot of people. Time spent reading CVs that turn out to be unsuitable seems to be a consistent complaint. It can however be reduced significantly by the use of some pretty simple steps:

Step 1

Don't read CVs as you receive them. Set a date and don't look at any CVs until you've hit that date. Gather all the CVs and read them all in one sitting. Make sure you are in the right frame of mind to carry out a review of the CVs. Don't do it if you're liable to get interrupted or distracted. I find I can review about thirty to forty CVs, certainly for an initial screen, in ten to fifteen minutes. This is important, as our judgement can be very dependent upon our mood. What might get past our review today may not pass tomorrow when we're feeling tired or irritable. Because of this, it's important to review each and every CV against a consistent set of criteria and in a uniform manner.

Step 2

Before you even look at a CV write down the key things you're looking for in the CV. This can be qualifications, type of experience, level of experience, evidence of certain characteristics or whatever is really important to you. Make sure it's a short list of the four to five really important factors.

This step helps to focus the mind on exactly what you're looking for. Make sure you physically write down these factors somewhere where you can keep referring back to them as you review the CVs. Reading CVs is one of the easiest ways to waste time and to allow your mind to wander, losing focus on what you're actually looking for in a CV.

Step 3

Now you're ready for the first pass. Scan the first two pages looking for evidence of your key factors. Look at the qualifications, read the summary, scan the last two or three roles. If you can't find evidence of at least three of your key factors reject the CV and move on. Don't fall into the trap of reading each one line-by-line. CVs can often be very interesting and why wouldn't they be: many can be wonderfully creative works of fiction! You can easily find yourself reading further out of curiosity or amusement, don't do it! This is the time wasting trap. Sitting with a pile of forty CVs means you must make a decision in less than 20 seconds; otherwise the job will take hours rather than minutes.

Step 4

As you find evidence for a key factor make a note of at the top of the CV with a tick if it looks good or a question mark if you're not sure. Keep the ones with three or more notes on the top. Bin the rest.

Step 5

Unless you're very lucky and have had a lot of very suitable applications this will generally have you down to somewhere between one and ten CVs. Now is the time when you can pay much more attention and start to rank each CV in terms of possible suitability. Write down the ten names on a sheet of paper. Review each CV again in terms of each key factor and give a rating from one to five, one being possibly of interest, 5 being definitely of interest. This is a very focused exercise. Don't allow yourself to spend too long reading each CV. You are simply rating them in terms of fit against each of your key factors. You have now successfully identified those that are of interest and you have ranked your top ten. Table 2 below shows an example of a shortlist rating.

If the CV's are being reviewed by more than one person, get each person to do the same thing. If you come up with the same shortlist that's an excellent sign that the group has a common understanding of what's required. Any major differences between the individual shortlists shows you that further discussions of your key criteria are required.

Name	Qualifications	Relevance of Technical Experience	Leadership Evidence	Customer Facing Experience	Total
A	3	4	3	2	12
B	5	2	2	1	10
C	3	3	1	3	10
D	1	3	1	1	6

Table 2 – Example of a short list rating table

Step 6

Ideally I would not recommend interviewing any more than five or six candidates. Of course you can always interview more if you really don't quite know what you're looking for and you've got the time to do so. I find interviewing any more than six people can make decision making difficult, as the differences between candidates can become blurred in terms of your decision making. In any shortlist you will generally have one or two real front runners. You will also have two or three solid candidates and maybe one or two outliers. Outliers are those you're not sure of, but who are worth interviewing just to make sure that your perceived favourites really are the right fit. It can be informative to interview candidates who are just outside of your ideal level of required ability in a key factor. By this I mean somebody who's maybe a little short of the required abilities, skills or experience and somebody who maybe has got a little more than you think you need. This can often help to ratify your final decision.

Step 7

By ranking the CVs prior to interview, you've automatically prioritised them. It's important to remember though this is just a ranking of your impression of their suitability from their CVs – this rating process is only used to select those candidates worth interviewing, no more, no less. They will certainly shift around in order of preference once you've interviewed them. If there's one consistent theme throughout the recruitment process it is that there is little correlation between CVs and interview performance. If CVs alone were an indicator of suitability for a role, we would have given up interviewing years ago. You definitely need to fight your instincts to favour the candidates with the strongest CVs. We'll discuss interviewing in more detail in Chapter 7 (Interviewing: getting the most out of the process) but it's absolutely crucial to remember that the CVs job is to convince you that the person is worth interviewing. Once that has been achieved, the CV merely serves as an aid to interviewing. It helps highlight areas that require further investigation.

So having completed the CV review process you've filtered your thirty or more CVs down to ten and then ranked the ten to allow you to pick your top five or six for interview. The process will have taken five minutes to identify your key factors, fifteen minutes to find those CVs that might be suitable, twenty minutes to review and rank those one to ten

CV's that are suitable. You should be finished in less than an hour. By following this process you will minimise your wasted time, you will judge each CV subjectively and fairly against the same criteria and you will come up with a strong shortlist of candidates for interview.

This is basically the process followed by all good professional recruiters. Granted the steps may sometimes be spread out, but in essence that's how professional recruiters manage their time in an efficient way. There are numerous software tools out there that help you to follow this process. They need you to define what you're after by setting search criteria based on keywords. Then they simply rate CVs by counting keywords and rating each CV based on a numerical score. It's as simple as that. By following the above steps you can achieve the same result. If you know what you're looking for you will be more effective than any piece of software. As good as the software is, it lacks the reasoning to figure out the intricacies of language. Without specific keywords within the text, it simply has no way of knowing that people often use different language to describe the same thing. This is why we hear frequent stories of eminently suitable candidates being rejected by a company's automated screening process. The automated process relies on the person setting the search term criteria having an awareness of all the possible keywords that may appear on suitable CVs. That's why I'm pretty dubious about total reliance on automated processes for all but the most simple of tasks. Any ambiguity with regards to keywords can cause mistakes and the worst sin of all - rejecting a suitable CV. This, unfortunately, frequently does happen.

Now you've shortlisted your candidates for interview, you're ready to go, right? Wrong – before the interview you will need to review each again. This time you will be thinking much more about where the perceived strengths and weaknesses lie. More on this in Chapter 7 (Interviewing: getting the most out of the process), when we discuss interview preparation. As you do this you need to ask yourself why the person is suitable – this will suggest some questions to verify whether you are right or not. You will also need to ask yourself whether you have any doubts about the ability of this person to do a good job. Again this thought process will suggest some further questions. If it's blindingly obvious that the person can do the job then you need to be looking at asking questions to identify why they would want to do the job. Figure 3 summarises the key steps in our short-listing process.

CV Short-listing Process

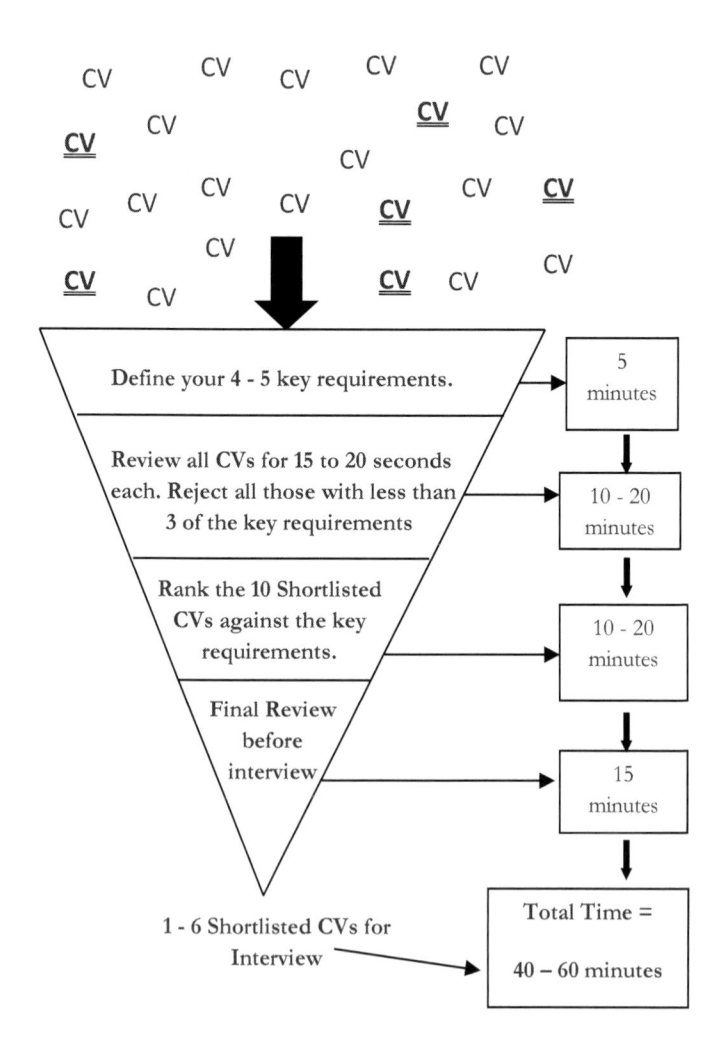

Define your 4 - 5 key requirements. — 5 minutes

Review all CVs for 15 to 20 seconds each. Reject all those with less than 3 of the key requirements — 10 - 20 minutes

Rank the 10 Shortlisted CVs against the key requirements. — 10 - 20 minutes

Final Review before interview — 15 minutes

1 - 6 Shortlisted CVs for Interview → Total Time = 40 – 60 minutes

Figure 3

General Guidelines on Reviewing CVs

Generally when we are recruiting new staff, we are really looking for people with a track record of successfully delivering things. These are the types of people in every organisation that get on with the job, deliver results, generally work well with others and help to ensure that things run smoothly. There are usually signs within a CV to indicate the type of characteristics and typical behaviours of the person. I believe the style of language used can really give a good insight into the way people work and the traits and characteristics associated with their personality and performance in a work environment. Those CVs that highlight an ability to do the job and to also improve the way things are done are worth seeking out and interviewing. Those that show evidence of delivering improvements, seeking out ways to improve and talking about improvements in important business metrics such as cost, customer satisfaction, etc, are the proactive types that every business needs.

It of course important to sense-check these claims at interview to make sure they are genuine. Let's face it, these days there's so much CV advice around that it's pretty easy for anybody to convey that they are a hard working and professional team player with great organisational and communication skills capable of taking on any challenge.

The point to bear in mind when reading the CV is that we're looking for evidence to suggest that the person is at least trying to show that they are a proactive achiever. They must convey an ability to deliver results and to make a positive contribution to the business. Failing to do this on a CV is a poor sign. It's the candidate's best opportunity to really sell themselves, win an interview and get the process going. CVs lacking in impact, that leave you wondering what are the person's actual unique abilities and strengths, are best consigned to the bin. In today's ultra-competitive job market a candidate failing to grasp the opportunity to sell themselves in the best possible way shows signs of laziness and apathy which don't auger well for their attitude to future job performance. How will such a person have the best interests of the business at heart if you were to hire them?

Red Flags and Green Lights on CVs

The following are some simple points that I have found to be clear indicators of a person's attitude to work and performance. Some may seem overly simplistic but they are designed to make you think about how the candidate has chosen to sell themselves to you. Are they seeking to impress you and create a positive selling proposition that makes you keen to meet and interview them? Are they merely going through the motions of providing you with the minimum amount of information, leaving the responsibility for making the decision entirely to you? Are they basically saying "here's what I've done, you decide if I'm any use to you or not?"

Red Flags

What warning signs should you look out for when reviewing CVs?

Responsibilities that have simply been cut and pasted onto a CV – this generally indicates a lazy attitude, an inability or unwillingness to explain what they do on a daily basis. Instead of taking the time to simply and concisely explain what they do and what their responsibilities are, such candidates simply think – why bother when I can just cut and paste a long list of my tasks and responsibilities.

Exaggerated achievements

This is always a real warning sign worthy of further investigation. Exaggerations can be a strong indicator of a dreamer or a person who lacks the ability to focus on single issues and deliver results. It's fine to be setting strategies and defining organisational development programmes for those few sitting in the upper echelons of an organisation. In the real world most of us are charged with managing specific items of work on a daily basis and actually making sure they get completed

Repetitive Text

This again suggest laziness. If you find yourself reading text describing a job that the candidate has done and it's exactly the same as a role they have done at a different organisation this would suggest that it's been lazily cut and pasted onto the CV. You need to ask how accurate a representation it is as regards what they've actually been doing.

Vague or insufficient language

If having read the description of the company and the role you can't figure out what the person actually did, reject the CV. If someone can't be bothered to make an effort to explain what they did in terms that anyone can understand it does not bode well. It suggests a devil-may-care, take-it-or-leave-it attitude. "Here I am, this is what I've done, it's your decision and your risk to decide whether to hire me or not."

Lack of achievements

This is one that I find amazing. Failing to highlight any achievements is really missing an opportunity on a CV. At any level of job you should always be looking to make things better and increase your contribution to the business. Why would anybody fail to mention some key achievements that they have delivered when doing their job?

Green Lights

So what are the good indicators to look out for that show us somebody is potentially a solid performer?

- A track record of winning awards and of being nominated for new projects, initiatives or teams suggests a history of delivery and performance

- A steady and consistent record of job promotions is always a good indicator of a strong performer, especially if it's happened in more than one organisation.

- A candidate spending the optimum length of time in a role is always a good sign. Generally three to four years is long enough in any one role. The typical cycle is:

Year 1 – learn the job requirements.

Year 2 – start to put your own stamp onto the role, challenging the way things are done and trying to deliver more for less commitment in terms of time or resources. In other words you're looking for evidence of the person progressing within the role, taking on more challenges and responsibilities and delivering more as they become more experienced.

Year 3 – transitioning out of the role – setting it up so that someone new can take over, making sure all the procedures and policies are in place.

Someone doing the same job year after year without making material improvements suggests a clock-watcher lacking in any real motivation to maximise their contribution. Of course sometimes a person's job title may stay the same, but they may have increased their responsibilities and contribution to the business over time. You really want to see evidence of somebody keen to develop themselves and to increase their levels of responsibility throughout their time in a role. Maybe they've worked for a small business that simply doesn't afford them the opportunity to change jobs every two to three years but you need to see evidence of increasing responsibility over time.

Of course these green flags need to be explored in greater detail during the interview process, but their presence on a CV suggests an achiever pattern and these are the types of people who will add the most value for you. Failure to find green light indicators would always put me off, unless of course the role is of the most menial and repetitive type, where initiative is not really required.

CHAPTER 6: SPREADING THE HIRING MESSAGE

We all know that lots of people find a new job via networking and through contacts. We often hear it reported that lots of jobs are never advertised and we hear about this almost mythical, secret world of the "unadvertised" job market. What does this mean? Put simply it means that often a company manages to fill a vacancy before they have advertised it. Usually this happens because they already know somebody who can do the job and, if luck is with them, that person is available and interested at the time that they need to fill the role.

In today's world of connectedness through social media tools, you must maximise your chances of finding suitable and interested candidates through every means possible. What I'm talking about here is building upon the tried and tested method of old-fashioned networking: telling your own direct contacts when you're looking to fill a position. Your aim is to extend this network to take advantage of how powerful our networks have become due to the far-reaching capabilities of social media. You know the old fashioned method of ringing around trusted colleagues and contacts works. You must use every possible additional communication channel at your disposal to let your contacts know that you're hiring and exactly what you're looking for. You don't need to bombard people. Often it's simply a case of "piggy backing" onto some other message that you're already exchanging with people. A simple one-liner to let people know you're hiring often makes people consider whether they might know somebody. If they do, they can read your requirements in detail and then forward it on, if it's suitable to do so.

It's very likely that somebody that you're connected with will know somebody suitable for a role you need to fill. You may not even know the contact well but if you're in the same geographical area or the same industry it's very likely they or one of their contacts will know somebody suitable. Think about it yourself from own your own perspective - how many people have you spoken to in the last month who told you that they're looking for a job or that their cousin or neighbour or son or daughter or whoever is looking for a job. This type of behaviour is very common for certain things we already do – for example how do we find tradesmen normally? We ask friends and neighbours and we go by recommendations. So this type of networking already works; you just need to maximise it to help spread your hiring message. People have grown accustomed to this type of approach. Just look at the rise in charity events that people participate in and how they spread the message about looking for sponsorship. We're used to seeing lots of messages about various things and if something crosses our path where we think we might have a solution, that's when we read the detail and pass it on if we think it's appropriate. The key thing is to keep the message short, snappy and to the point. Make sure it's informative and that it will make sense to somebody who might have the answer to what you're looking for. Once it catches their eye they need a simple link to more detailed background information. And remember it has to be easy to forward on to somebody else and it must be straight forward for them to actually apply for the position.

Examples of how to spread your hiring message

Today's social media tools give us numerous easy and free ways to spread a message. Let's look at some examples:

Email signatures

Your email signature will allow you to put in one-liner like: "we're looking to hire a new accounts receivable officer". We can also add a hyperlink which allows any interested party to click the link and see the details. Even if you don't have a company website or careers section there are numerous free online job boards which allow you to post job adverts for free. Now you may never get a suitable applicant through the website itself but that's OK, you just need a suitable means of sharing and showing the job details displayed in a professional manner. A simple web-link of this type can be very easily distributed without having to worry about attachments, firewalls, etc. A link to a publicly known and safe website will allow instant transmittal of your vacancy details that other people can very easily pass on. A quick search on Google for "free employer job advertising" will throw up numerous options that you can use.

Alternatively, there are also numerous free file-sharing services out there. These allow you to create or upload a document, such as your job or person specification. You will then be able to share a web-link that allows others to view the document. With so many people using mobile technology to share things, using a link is definitely the best option, as they are very reliable and very easy to share. Trying to distribute attachments (documents containing job specifications and advert details) is unreliable and should be avoided

LinkedIn

Your profile allows for status updates which all your contacts will see. Again a simple update with a link to a job advert lets everybody in your network know that you're hiring.

Skype

Your account allows you to put a message onto your profile which can be viewed by your contacts, or you can select it to be viewed on your public profile.

Targeted emails

Why not send a general email to all your contacts with a brief message letting them know you're hiring.

Non-business related social networking sites

It's very simple to post an update on any non-business social networking sites you frequent, such as Facebook, etc.

YouTube

Why not record a short video of yourself or others talking about your company, what you're trying to do and some discussion of what you're looking for in a new hire. You can embed a link to your job within the text accompanying the video. Again this is something that people can very easily share and it can really be a very useful tool in promoting the culture within your company. This is something that's very hard to capture on paper but can be very well conveyed by a good speaker.

Free publicity

Contact your local paper and let them know that you're hiring. They may be interested in doing an article on your business or adding some information about your business into an upcoming article. Also consider talking to trade associations and professional bodies; their press secretaries and editors are always on the lookout for material to publish. Once such stories have been produced you can share these across all the available social media platforms. This type of approach can be very effective. Most articles are now also available in an online format so you can easily share a link with your network. This is an increasingly popular tool, as people very often join networks specifically with the intention of tapping into information-sharing streams.

Basically it's the power of your secondary connections through social media that really allows you to massively extend your network and spread your message. In the past we might have told ten or twenty people, who could go on to tell two or three other people who they think might be interested – total audience thirty to forty people. Messages transmitted through today's media tools can easily be seen by thousands of people. Let's say your email signature has the same message so that every single contact that you email will know that you're hiring. If they like you they will typically stop and think about someone they might know or about how they might help you find somebody suitable. Alternatively, of course, they may think about how getting a job may help somebody they know. So in this case they're more likely to forward the message on even if they're unsure about whether the person is looking or even about whether they might be interested or not. In fact it's well known that when using social media it's not necessarily your primary connections but your secondary connections that are most likely to yield positive referrals. The numbers can stack up pretty quickly – let's say thirty contacts send it on to three of their contacts who'll probably forward it to three of their contacts and so on. The numbers viewing the initial message can reach several hundred very quickly.

You also need to consider using any general business communication tools that get distributed: newsletters, announcements, trade magazine articles, website updates, product videos, press releases. Anything of this nature, which people are already reading, needs to be considered as a suitable medium to transmit your hiring message.

CHAPTER 7: INTERVIEWING - GETTING THE MOST OUT OF THE PROCESS

The best interviewer I have ever encountered followed a very logical and thorough process and asked some very good open but probing questions. He listened to every single word I said and I knew this as he demonstrated it by asking good probing questions after I'd spoken. He also clearly demonstrated active listening characteristics. After the interview I felt that he'd obtained a very thorough understanding of my strengths and weakness and what I was capable of doing. As I walked back to the car after the interview I also wondered how he felt I'd performed as a candidate. As I thought about it I realised I had no idea how he felt about it. He did not betray any signals or signs about how he felt about any of my answers other than to offer words of encouragement for me to continue talking. I think this is really the aim of the interview: to find out what the interviewee is really like, how they work and what their strengths and weaknesses are.

I find a lot of people approach interviews thinking they have to trip the interviewee up in some way, trying to catch them out with some lie or exaggeration. Yes, that can happen, but there's little point in approaching interviews in a confrontational way, as that will merely force the interviewee to behave in a withdrawn and guarded manner. Your aim should be to allow the interviewee to give an honest and open account of themselves so that you can form a judgement based on everything you've seen and heard during the interview. During interviews, the interviewee should be talking for at least eighty percent of the time. You may give an overview, of course, about the company and the role, but otherwise you should be asking questions and listening very carefully. It's vital that you pay attention to watch out for any cues signalling areas requiring further investigation.

Testing commitment

The first point to consider about interviews is actually setting them up. This simple task can often give a good indication of someone's genuine interest or motivation in exploring opportunities with your business. This can be particularly relevant when you're dealing with passive candidates. Yes they're potentially interested in opportunities, but when pushed to do so they are unable to find time to schedule an interview during business hours. Now I'm not saying you should be impolite and push somebody to take a short notice interview. Doing this would suggest a disorganised and inflexible culture within your company. It can also convey a degree of panic where the person taking the role is less important than the fact that it must be filled by a certain date.

It is important that you convey the fact that you are treating the hiring process with the required degree of seriousness. If your behaviour and actions suggest that filling the role is just a nuisance to you, then you're unlikely to fill the position with a strong candidate. In my experience, pretty much any job can become a major difficulty for you if it's being done by somebody who turns out to be a poor performer. You don't get what you pay for and poor performance can be very damaging to team morale, the customer experience and overall business performance.

So the main point is that you should approach the logistics of the hiring process in a way that says: "this is an important role for us, we need to fill it within certain timescales but the most important point is that we fill it with the right person who will do a good job." If you encounter a situation where a candidate is not making themselves available then you should walk away. Send a simple note stating: "thanks for your interest but we have other suitable candidates who can make themselves available and we are going to proceed with them instead." If you've failed to set a date having offered two or three options you can safely assume that the person is really not that interested in joining your business. It's far better to find out at the early stages before you've committed time and energy to detailed discussions with them. It can be very frustrating to only find out the real extent of their interest when you actually offer them a job.

Offer any more than two or three options and you're being too accommodating, unless there's a genuine issue, such as illness or somebody is just about to go off on a trip or a holiday. The key thing is to offer some reasonable options, and to set something up quickly. It's important at this stage to get the candidate to show commitment. Somebody looking to do an interview outside of work hours does not sound very committed and would certainly put me off proceeding with them.

There's a fine line to tread: be reasonable and flexible to some degree (particularly if it's a rare and valuable type of candidate) but make sure that you are seeing a commitment to the process right from the start. If you are unable to get that commitment, that's an early warning sign that the candidate is not really serious.

Reasons for conducting interviews

Interviewers often approach an interview with a single objective and treat the process as a very one-dimensional affair. The mindset is "can this person do the job for me?" If you approach the process with an open and inquisitive mind there's a lot we can learn from interviews. There are actually several reasons why we interview people as outlined below:

- To assess the suitability of a candidate for a specific job opening.

- To assess the potential fit of a candidate to your company culture.

- To use the opportunity to learn from the candidate. Things like market information, business development opportunities, examples of best practice or success stories from other businesses, benchmarking of other businesses, for example, can all be discussed during interviews. You often learn much more about what's really going on somewhere during a face to face discussion of issues than you can from other sources.

- To project your company in the best possible light and help facilitate possible future business opportunities. Today's candidate may be tomorrow's buyer, customer or supplier. It's a small world and interviews give a real window to the outside world of what your company is really like. Make sure you take that opportunity to sell a positive image of yourself and your business.

Effective preparation for interviewers

This is a crucial step that many interviewers neglect and it always reflects badly on somebody if they have failed to prepare. It's particularly poor, considering that adequate preparation only takes about ten to fifteen minutes. Arriving to an interview and spending the first few minutes reading the CV is not making best use of interview time. It also suggests that it's the first time you've done so, not a good thing to portray, particularly if it's a good candidate that you'd like to try and impress. Being rude or off-hand in an interview serves no purpose whatsoever and can do damage to the reputation of your business. It's important therefore to make sure that you don't unintentionally offend somebody by making it obvious that you haven't bothered to do any preparation.

Before meeting the person you need to review the CV. Outline what specific areas of the candidate's experience you wish to explore and what specific questions you want to get answers to - make notes or bullets point on the CV to serve as a reminder for your questions. It's absolutely fine to have a CV with handwritten notes on it. It shows you have prepared for the meeting and that of course you've actually read their CV. I find this very important – you really need to have your full attention focused on what the person is saying, how they're behaving and of course what they're not saying. It can be difficult to focus on the answers when your brain is occupied with thinking about the next set of questions. That's why it really helps to have reminder notes actually written in front of you. That way you can relax and listen to the answers and allow yourself to process what you're hearing. You can feel safe in the knowledge that when the person is finished and you've exhausted the particular point you can just refer to your notes to remind of your next line of questioning. This makes you look competent as an interviewer as you're obviously listening in an active manner. You are also completely focused on the answers you're getting and you're sticking to an interview plan which puts you in a position of control. Frequently people make the mistake of asking an initial open question such as "tell me about your current role". While that question is being answered they are frantically reading through the rest of the CV trying to identify a second question. This is blatantly obvious to an interviewee and presents a poor image. The lack of eye contact is off-putting and everybody knows you can't read and listen at the same time, not properly anyway. To be in a position where you are conducting an interview but you are obviously not listening to what the interviewee is saying is poor practice and needs to be avoided. Good preparation will allow you to have a plan in place to ensure that you get an answer to all of the key questions you need to ask.

Interview format advice

Firstly thank the candidate for attending the interview and make them feel at ease; the offer of coffee or water also helps. Explain the purpose of the meeting and who all the attendees are. Explain what each of the interviewers does and what your own role is within the business. I find it best to give a brief overview of the business and what the future plans are. This will take five to ten minutes. While you are providing the overview it helps to let the person settle in and to overcome any initial nerves. A little nervousness in a candidate is perfectly normal; in fact it's usually a good sign. You don't want to get a poor first impression just because the candidate is nervous and if you initiate the proceedings and give a bit of background information it definitely puts them a little more at ease. It is also good practice to explain what you specifically want to achieve from the interview. Launching straight into direct questioning can be off-putting to many people. Clarify the basic structure that you will follow and offer the chance to ask questions. Questions are often reserved for the end of the interview but should also be encouraged during the interview if clarification of any point is required. It's always very useful to explain the basic logistics of the role up front just to clarify that everybody's on the same page. It's always best to clear up any misunderstandings early and encouraging questions throughout the interview helps with this.

Ask the candidate how much they already know about the business and if there are any key points that they would like to discuss. The best way to start an interview is to ask some good open questions and let the candidate talk before probing in greater depth by asking detailed questions. Asking open questions and letting them talk before asking detailed questions is also a good way of putting a candidate at ease. They will be more honest when they are allowed to feel at ease and will feel that they can speak freely. Encouraging the person to speak freely and be open and honest with you is the aim of the game.

As an interviewer it's very important to <u>not react</u> openly to what's being said. If a candidate senses that you don't like the answer they're giving then they'll start to veer in different directions and will start to give you the answers that they believe that you want to hear. It's worth remembering that some people can interview extremely well but be poor performers in the (actual) job. Don't allow yourself to be fooled by somebody telling you what you want to hear. If you don't like the answer you hear, make a mental note and move on to the next question without showing a negative response. You should actively listen and ensure that the interviewee knows that you've heard what they're saying without allowing the person to steer the conversation in one direction or another. We all learn to adapt our behavior at a very young age and we also develop manipulative traits at a young age. When faced with an interviewer who is clearly not happy with the answers they're getting, a candidate will shift their response to say what they think you want to hear. This is particularly true if we're very keen to be offered a job. As an interviewer it's your job to make sure that the person is encouraged to talk and to give open and honest answers. We may not like what we're hearing but that will be used in our final decision making process after the interview.

Interview questions – the best ones to use and those best avoided

In general terms it's best to keep questions as simple and straightforward as possible, especially at the beginning of the interview. Your job as an interviewer is to facilitate the candidate answering questions in an open and honest way. You need to use the answers to form your judgment, verifying whenever required by seeking clarification. You must reserve your final judgment until after the interview has been completed.

> Tip: You must resist the urge to form a first impression at the beginning of the interview! You must wait until you are at least half way through before you begin to form any judgment.

Human nature dictates that we form first impressions very quickly, some say it happens within seven seconds. Forming a judgment on somebody's suitability to do a job and to assess how they might fit within your culture, based on their traits, characteristics and style of working, definitely cannot be judged within seven seconds! You need to fight your in-built tendency to form some sort of first impression. Why? Because it's unfair on the interviewee and it's often very wrong. Before you even start the interview you will have some pre-conceptions based on the CV and often these will be dead wrong. Our brain is programmed to form some sort of short term decision in this type of situation, so it's actively looking for clues to suggest certain things about the person. If you're starting to form a first impression then you will be inclined to start asking questions to reinforce your bias. You must fight this tendency and in the first half of the interview it's best to just let the person talk. Let the interviewee explain what they've been doing in their own words. Only ask open questions:

"Why did you decide to take a job like that?"

"Why did your boss ask you to do that project?"

"How did you feel when they gave you that extra responsibility?"

"What did you enjoy most about that job?"

"What did you enjoy least about that job?"

"Why did you enjoy working for that manager?"

Once you have allowed the interviewee some time to explain things in their own words, common themes will appear, evidence of behavior patterns will become apparent and if you've listened properly you will have seen several flags that require further investigation. These can be both red and green flags which will be suggestive of underlying behaviors and job performance capabilities. In the early phase of the interview don't interrupt the person. Simply make a brief note about a question that you want to ask and continue listening.

Once you've spent enough time listening, it's time to start probing what you've heard. You've given the person ample opportunity to describe who they are and how they work. Now you can start to challenge, probe and get a deeper understanding of their real strengths and weaknesses.

Probing questions can be both open and closed. Here are some good examples:

"Why did you do it that way?"

"Did you consider any other options?"

"How did other team members feel when you took that decision?"

"Tell me how you managed to get that improvement in the sales figures?"

"What was the long term impact of doing things that way?"

Remember that the person may turn out to be unsuitable for the current position, but could be the perfect candidate for a new role that you might have in the future. If you start to ask probing questions too soon in the interview, you interrupt their flow, which may make the interviewee hesitant and guarded. You may not believe what they're saying but that may be your own bias clouding your judgment. You need to give them the opportunity to convince you that it's true. If after that, you remain unconvinced then that is a fair decision based on the evidence that's in front of you. For example, somebody claiming to have made significant improvements, but who is not really able to explain in any detail exactly how those improvements were specifically made, is probably exaggerating their own personal input. This is the point where the details contained in the CV needs to be explored to ensure the person can demonstrate a really good understanding and is very clear on the detail contained within it.

If you show frustration or disappointment at any of the answers during the interview you will generally close the dialogue down and lose the opportunity to gain any further information. Try to avoid the temptation to allow your judgment to be biased by personal likes or dislikes and preconceptions. It's a common mistake to pre-judge a candidate and then to spend the interview looking for evidence to support your opinion. Remember to keep the first half of the interview open and practise active listening. Once the person has had a fair chance to explain themselves, switch to a more probing style. Let's talk a little more about the types of questions you can use:

Open Questions

General open questions are good conversation starters and help to make people feel at ease. They encourage interviewees to explain things in their own words. Use of good general open questions will give you a good sense of the type of person that's sitting in front of you. Examples include:

> "What's the current situation with your-self?"

> "What do you know about our company?"

> "What made you choose that as a career option?"

Closed Questions

These should only really be used when looking for specific information; overuse can kill the conversation and make an interview feel like an interrogation. They are best used sparingly, as they often stop a conversation in its tracks. Examples include:

> "So you have no experience of using CAD packages?"

> "How many people did you directly manage?"

> "Who was your customer contact for that project?"

Leading questions

These should really be avoided, unless you're trying to make a very specific point. They can appear aggressive and offensive. They are very suggestive of bias on the interviewer's part and this is never a good thing. If you find yourself asking a leading question then you're looking for a specific answer. Why? You need to stop yourself and try to ask a more open question that allows the interviewee to give their own answer – it's their interview after all! Examples include:

> **"So you wouldn't be interested in work like that would you?"**
>
> **"Are you suggesting that confrontation is a good thing?"**
>
> **"Are you telling me that you struggle with complexity?**
>
> **"So have you struggled with that type of situation?"**
>
> **"This role requires excellent time management skills, are you OK working to strict deadlines?"**

Each of these questions could be asked in a more open manner and this would be more likely to give you an answer that reflects how the person reacts or behaves in certain situations. You may indeed conclude that an interviewee struggles in a certain area but it's rare that they will come straight out and admit it, if you're leading towards that answer. The response to open questions like:

> "How do you typically react when faced with complex situations?"
>
> "How do you ensure all your tasks are done on time?"

will tell you a lot more about the person than a closed question. Closed questions really force the person into a one word answer, whereas open questions force them to describe what they actually do to deal with certain issues. A lack of conviction in the answer can betray a strong possibility that, for example, there's an inability to deal with complexity or to work to deadlines.

Multiple questions

This is another type of question that should be avoided. Multiple questions tend to be asked in an effort to a get a quick overall impression and betray a rushed approach. They cause confusion and people will only answer part of the question that you've asked them. They need to be split into individual questions and asked one at a time. Examples include:

"Why do you want to leave your current job and why would we want to hire you for this job?"

"Have you any people management skills and if so how would you normally deal with an under-performing employee?"

Competency based questions

If you are conducting a competency based assessment, you can find a lot of good tips online, where there is a vast array of good sample questions available to help you in assessing a candidate's suitability. Remember that when using closed competency based questions you are also demonstrating your knowledge and expertise in a particular area. Preparation helps a lot in conducting a successful interview and ensures that both parties get a positive impression of each other. Good examples would include:

"Tell me about a time when you had to solve a complex problem – what did you do to fix it?

"Give me an example that shows me that you are comfortable working as part of a team?

"Describe how you dealt with an awkward colleague who refused to help you?"

"Give me an example of when you personally identified an issue that needed to be fixed and what you did to resolve the issue?"

Make sure that the candidate gives you a clear answer about what they (personally) specifically did.

Red Flags – warning signs and deceptive behaviors to look out for

The subject of lying and how to spot when people are lying is a large and complex issue. In my experience a good thing to look out for are red flags which betray possible deceptive behaviour. Potential deceptive behavior in an interview is a clear warning sign and should always be explored fully to make sure that you get a clear explanation. If you are unable to get a clear answer then you need to be wary of hiring that person. If you feel you can't get a level of trust from an interviewee, why would you take the risk of actually employing that person?

Body language is complex and you can't get a handle on someone's body language habits and traits during a one hour interview, but you can look out for obvious red flags. Two warning signs together, such as a nervous laugh combined with someone sitting back in their seat, would indicate potential deceptive behaviour. Make sure to pay attention to non-verbal responses when you pose probing questions. Most people betray their discomfort unconsciously to some degree and when you see the signs this is your cue to really explore the issue in detail. If a candidate is not prepared to go into full details that always rings alarm bells for me. You may not resolve the issue fully in the interview, of course, but speaking to referees afterwards to verify employment dates, responsibilities, reporting lines and actual job performance can be used to put your mind at rest or to highlight a particular problem area.

Common lies or deceptions uncovered during the interview process

Dates of employment

People often try to make their employment record appear to be more stable than it actually is. Incorrect or confusing dates can be indicative of something to hide. In general I would advise that you always state during an interview that it's your policy to check with each and every employer to verify employment dates, job titles and responsibilities for any potential new recruit. You should ask the interviewee if they are OK with this and watch their response very carefully. Anything less than a positive response can indicate that there might be something to hide. You can explore any hesitation by asking if any of the candidate's previous employers would be happy to confirm any of the details you've discussed and if they would be happy to recommend them.

Embellished or exaggerated responsibilities and/or achievements

Generally you can pick up on this in interview if the candidate is less than credible when explaining the details. Another approach is to ask:

> **"It's our policy to always speak to references for any new hire. What would your references say about what you've told us today?"**

Watch the reaction closely to this type of question; it is very telling if somebody starts to backtrack.

Job titles and reporting relationships

If you suspect something doesn't quite ring true you can let the candidate know that you will be checking detailed references. Be careful here though, as sometimes people can be deliberately deceptive by giving the name of a former colleague or friend who will pretend that they were the candidate's boss. If in doubt, a quick search of the company's website or LinkedIn may confirm who's who. Failing that, call the company directly and seek clarification. In over ten years of doing so, I've never encountered any difficulty in terms of getting co-operation when verifying reference details. People are always happy to help you make sure your due diligence process can be completed.

Qualifications

This is probably the easiest area in which to be deceptive. All qualifications should be checked or verified. Lots of professional bodies now provide reference numbers where a quick online check can match personal details to a qualification number. Failing that most institutions and professional bodies are happy to provide a confirmation of some sort, for a small fee. It is money well spent as far as I'm concerned as hiring somebody who's prepared to fake their qualifications is always going to end in tears. A common trick is to state qualifications when in fact only part of a course has been completed. The candidate may well have attended part of the course but never actually completed it. There are a lot of online training materials these days and what may appear to be a good qualification may have been attained in two hours simply by watching some online content. If you don't know of the qualification already always ask what was involved in gaining the qualification, who was the awarding body and how long it took to complete. It's also worth asking what was required to get the actual qualification – were there exams or assignments?

Others

There's a variety of other things that people do in order to present themselves in a positive light. You should be aware that people will actually put down fake companies, or add companies that they've never actually worked for. They may fake sporting achievements or claim they've won awards to make them look good. I find it's always worth asking some very detailed questions about such claims. A lack of familiarity with the details can be suggestive of deceptive behavior by the interviewee. This type of thorough questioning of specific details is a common technique used by police interrogators. It helps them to identify when people are lying about events that have taken place. If the person is lying it can be difficult for them to remain consistent in their answers and contradictions appear.

If you really need to explore any particular detail or issue during an interview don't be afraid to push the interviewee to the point where you can see that they're struggling or don't know the answer and see what happens. It can be very telling to watch the person's reaction in such a situation and you need to be convinced of the answers to feel confident in your decision making. It is easy enough when we know the person – we all generally know when close friends or family members are being less than truthful – they show their signals or red flags, the raised tone of voice, the lack of eye contact, etc. I don't recommend conducting interviews in the style of an interrogation, but I do recommend that you keep a keen eye open for any red flags that do occur and make sure to explore any issues that arise in full detail. Some people are very good at lying and remember that you simply may not catch them out, but there are other tools out there to help you, such as reference or qualification checks.

How to close the interview

Remember to take notes documenting all of the key information that you'll need later in the process. It's good practice to keep notes that would allow you to give a summary of the interview to a third party. It's also helpful to be able to refer back to previous notes during any further interviews, during the offer process or if you are required to provide feedback to the interviewee or somebody else at some future point. Remember to make sure that you have a good clear understanding of the key points.

Key information to make note of during interviews

- Why is the candidate looking for work?

- What is their availability to start a new role?

Are there any restrictions on them taking up a new role such as non-compete clauses, penalty clauses, payback of previous benefits or lost opportunity costs such as impending bonuses?

Are there any specific personal circumstances that came up during the interview that need to be considered?

- Why are they a good fit for the role?

- Why are they a good fit to your company culture?

Concluding the interview

Agree any action points and conclude the meeting making sure that they've had the opportunity to ask questions. Make sure to ask if they are still interested in working for you at the end of the interview. If they've uncovered any issues that would stop them taking a job with you, it's a good point to investigate what these are. Don't just assume that they're still interested. Let them know what the next step will be and when they will hear about the result of the interview. If the situation changes and there is no longer a role, tell the candidate. The number one complaint from candidates regarding interviews is lack of feedback. You can distinguish yourself and the company by always giving feedback, particularly honest feedback. If somebody interviewed particular poorly and you don't wish to be unkind, just let them know the result and offer them the chance to speak about it. It's easier to be honest in a conversation than getting involved in long drawn out emails. Of course it's also more difficult for someone to bring any type of bias or discrimination case against you if you've just given them some honest verbal feedback.

This type of closing question can really catch people off-guard and you can often hear a surprising range of remarkable stories that come to light, for example criminal convictions etc. You must not react to any story that comes up. Simply take a note and make sure to use it as part of your final decision making process.

CHAPTER 8: MANAGING THE OFFER PROCESS

This is one of the key steps in the hiring process in the sense that it's often where things go wrong. This can be very frustrating as it occurs right at the end, just at the point where you're hoping for a positive result. It's important to realise that the manner in which the offer process is handled can be a decisive factor in the decision making process for the candidate. It acts as a window into the organisation and often reflects the values and culture of your organisation. The way in which things are managed frequently puts candidates off actually accepting a job offer, even if it's a good offer. Common reasons that candidates state for rejecting job offers include employers being overly aggressive during negotiations, being overly pushy when looking for a decision, being perceived as being stubborn and inflexible when negotiating and not explaining the reasons behind negotiation decisions.

When conducting any package or salary negotiations you need to make sure that any discussions are carried out in an organised way. It is not a fair or reasonable strategy to suddenly start discussions when someone's not expecting it. The tone should be one of:

> "I want to have a call with you to discuss the terms and conditions of our offer – when is a good time for you to do this?"

Do not apply unnecessary pressure in terms of time-scale. The situation is already stressful enough. It's good to put timescales and deadlines in place, but make them realistic and reasonable. Agree up front with the candidate when they will give you a decision.

Preparation is the key in all negotiations, I learned this pretty quickly when negotiating job offers with people. No matter the experience or level of role, we all work for a salary, so it's an important issue and you need to get it right. When it comes to hiring it's always better to achieve a win-win type scenario. If either side feels hard done by, it is definitely going to manifest itself in difficulties further down the line. There are a number of key factors that are important to understand before you make your offer to a potential new hire:

What's the typical market rate for this specific vacancy or for similar types of vacancy? You need to benchmark against the market rates.

- How good is the person you're looking to hire when judged against this benchmark?

- How much do you need or want the person you're looking to hire?

- What are the current job-market conditions?

If there's a shortage of the type of person you're looking for you'll need to make sure that's reflected in the package that you offer. It's good to know the typical market rates but these may have to be exceeded in times of skills shortages.

A lot of this work can of course be done before you even find a potential candidate that you'd like to hire. It really helps to get the facts lined up before the process starts, because it can get a bit fraught at times and keeping an objective approach works wonders. The successful negotiation of an employment package is all about reaching a win-win situation as soon as possible. Remember there are numerous facets of a job offer including:

- Salary

- Performance bonus

- Profit share

- Relocation allowance or support

- Health insurance

- Life insurance

- Share options

- Pension

- Introductory bonus

- Educational supports

- Working hours

- Company car or car allowance

- Childcare support

People often get fixated on salary and while it's often the biggest single element it's certainly not the be all and end all. Rising income taxes across Europe means that every pound or euro earned to pay for something is often worth almost twice in gross salary terms. So just raising the salary being offered can be an expensive option for both parties. Personally I would always make sure that a candidate knows the full range of benefits on offer before I would discuss any changes to the salary. Often you can negotiate on salary, agreeing a number, only for a candidate to then start negotiating again on other elements of the offer. Or you may give in to salary requests when in fact the person may have settled for less money, once the full package is taken into consideration.

It's good practise to seek justification for any requested increase in offer. If a candidate genuinely wants to work for you, but it's going to cost them more in travel and childcare costs, you're very unlikely to get them to accept your offer. If a candidate is able to lay out a clear explanation and justification as to why your offer is unacceptable then you have something to work with. If the candidate is unwilling or unable to justify a hard and fast reason for their demands, I would advise you to leave the offer as it stands and see what happens – it's take it or leave it time. We'll cover the justification of demands in more detail shortly, but first we need to look at how we will actually start the negotiation process.

How to start the negotiation process

So where do we start? The point at which we begin negotiating can vary quite a lot. Generally all negotiations will involve an anchor point – this can be defined as a reference point around which any negotiations will revolve. The anchor point is often the first offer that is presented. You need to choose your anchor point wisely, as it will be referred to frequently during the process. Once it's been agreed, as the name suggests, it's pretty much fixed. Both parties will have a desire to define a different anchor and again it's very important to have done your homework.

If it's an advertised role with a stated salary or salary range and the person has applied then it's pretty straightforward. You can make a judgement on their suitability and experience or whatever criteria you judge as being most critical to your needs and make an offer that's appropriate to how they fit the scale you've used. Remember to always leave yourself some room for negotiation. It's very common for candidates to push back on the first offer made so you really need to be expecting to uplift your first offer by anything from three up to twenty percent. Most candidates expect this, so you need to be prepared and always leave some room for negotiation.

A little online research will give you some figures in terms of market salaries. When setting an anchor point, I would use factual evidence to justify where I've found this anchor point. Being able to explain that you've assessed the market and have found similar companies generally pay between x and y for this level of position or experience is useful information. This sets a clear target that you are hoping to hit and gives the candidate a clear indication that you are an organised and informed negotiator. There's a surprising amount of information available online: search for "job title" AND "salary" and you'll find free salary surveys, as well as anonymous salary info posted by employees on employment review sites. Public service and academic salaries are often published and freely available. Discussion groups often have online chats between groups of people openly talking about salaries and packages. If you're struggling, make sure to make use of your network. Trade associations, industry bodies, etc. may well have some data that can help you out. Recruitment companies can also advise you or you can engage them directly to conduct a tailored salary survey for you.

I generally find that, on both sides of the fence, being able to justify your position in a negotiation discussion really helps to keep things on a professional and productive footing. People can get annoyed or frustrated when they are unable to understand the other side's position. I would strongly advise against the use of entrenched or stubborn positions; this is very off putting to candidates. Even the perception that you are acting out of stubbornness can cause a candidate to reject your offer. Taking an overly strong or aggressive position can often work in certain types of negotiation situations but when it comes to hiring negotiations you must remember that ultimately you're trying to establish a long term employer/employee relationship. If it can't be started off on a positive footing of trust then it probably won't happen at all. The same counts of course with candidates who refuse to engage and just stubbornly make demands. These types of people are best avoided, I find.

If you're unsure of what you need to offer, you can of course always ask a candidate what they're looking for. This can often be the case if you're dealing with a passive candidate. It may seem a strange approach, but actually if somebody is really serious about taking up a new role they will certainly have given some serious consideration to what they'd be expecting in order to accept an offer. A good question to use:

"So what sort of salary and package would we need to offer you in order for you to be happy to accept a job with us?"

This actually leaves the door wide open but firmly puts the ball into the candidate's court to justify a package. I would issue this given the provision that maybe they can take a day or two to come back with a response. Always put a deadline on it. You then have something to discuss once they come back to you with a response and it puts pressure on the candidate to explain why they've come up with the numbers. Some people feel it's essential to know the current or previous salary and, yes, it's beneficial to have, but it's not necessarily going to help us. If the candidate was underpaid in their previous role they may not want to reveal the salary as it puts them in a weaker negotiating position. So if a candidate is clearly uncomfortable stating it, there's little point in pushing too hard. You can safely assume that they were probably underpaid or felt undervalued. If the candidate states a salary which is higher then you expected or seems a little over inflated, you can set and communicate your anchor point based on your earlier research. This shows you've done your research and justifies a good point at which to commence negotiations.

What's the best way to handle negotiation with a potential new hire?

Firstly define the anchor point. You can try to ascertain the candidate's current salary if possible, or define the salary range on offer to them directly to make sure you won't be wasting time, or do some research / external benchmarking to define a suitable range. Wherever you get your anchor point from, you need to confirm it to the candidate when you want to offer them a job. Doing so before this point doesn't really help. It can appear pushy and negative, and frankly sometimes tight-fisted if the money topic comes up too early in the process. It suggests that it's maybe a problem area and nobody wants to work for a company with money problems. You also need to know how good the candidate is and you don't really know that until the full interviewing process has been completed. It's far better to project oneself as a successful and financially healthy business with a prudent and informed approach to managing financial negotiations. These types of companies generally make the best employers.

When defining your position it's best to explain that it is based on market rates and other such independent sources. Simply telling people that the salary is "x" and no higher because of the salaries of existing employees is not a good reason. The person you're looking to hire may be more qualified or experienced or (frankly) better than existing employees. Using current internal salaries is something you clearly have to be mindful of in a wider business sense. It is, however, an inappropriate anchor point to communicate during your salary negotiations as it may deter your preferred candidate if they believe you can't afford them. It's not unusual, when you go out into the external market to hire somebody new to find that your current salaries are now out of sync with market rates. Trying to persuade somebody to accept an offer which is below the market rate can be difficult, especially if they're good at their job!

As regards negotiating, I've always found that it's good practise to be flexible and receptive to discussions and to demonstrate that you're prepared to listen and consider possible options. At the same time, of course, you must remain firm and stay in control. If somebody is not happy to accept your offer, get them to define exactly what they need to accept your offer. If you can arrange to do so, then make one counter-offer and see what happens. Beware the candidate that asks for something and once they've got it they subsequently ask for something else. This can often lead down the road of difficult and protracted negotiations, which ultimately fail and leave you having to start all over again. It's always good to have some choice if at all possible. Ideally have two candidates. Sort and offer quickly with the first and if it fails you have a second option. It's advisable to make an offer, agree some time for the person to consider things and agree a deadline as to when you'll talk again. It's important to clarify up front what's acceptable and what part of the offer needs to be improved. This helps, as it prevents the candidate from making excessive demands for each and every part of the package. Explain politely which items are fixed and cannot be changed and then agree which specific items will be negotiated. I would generally only recommend making one or two amended offers at most. If the person is still making further demands having already received two updated offers, there's a strong likelihood that they won't accept and you're best to call "final offer" at that point.

Personally I have rarely done salary negotiations face-to-face unless time really was a key pressure point. As soon as you know you want to offer, it's a good idea to confirm to the person that you're looking to progress. This is beneficial in terms of managing effective communication and also managing expectations. Letting the candidate know that there's an offer on the way makes them think about what they might get offered and what they need to be offered in terms of accepting it. Getting a candidate to focus their mind on this aspect of negotiations is important. I believe it's important to give the candidate the time and latitude to define what's important to them in terms of how they'll conduct negotiations. In terms of negotiating styles my experience has been that most people behave in a logical and reasonable manner when negotiating job offers. It's vital to remember that both sides need to engineer a win-win situation. Winning more than they need to on either side doesn't really generate any long term benefits. A short term win for an employer can quickly manifest itself in excessive future salary demands once the candidate becomes an employee. This can often happen just at the point where the person is becoming really useful to the business.

For example, taking advantage of the fact that somebody is desperate for a job and needs the money can present a temptation to offer them less than the market rate, knowing that they pretty much have to accept. Similarly some candidates can really force the negotiations because they think you have no other option because of a skills shortage. Such tactics can yield short term gain but also build resentment and will lead to problems further down the line. It's advisable to always approach salary negotiations from a win-win perspective. Even if you are unable to accede to demands, it's important to give the person the chance to make them and it's wise to consider any such demands within the right context. Some candidates view the salary negotiation process as an opportunity to really sell their capabilities and to keep pushing for as much as they can possibly get. Such tactics can reflect negatively on a candidate, but it's best to politely decline and make the case for why you're offering what you're offering. If people can see the reasons and logic behind your offer and can see that it's based on sound business principles, then that will reflect well on you as an employer and may help to swing things in your favour in the decision-making process. Not many people want to work for a financially irresponsible employer who could go out of business at any time.

Some candidates take a confrontational and aggressive stance or style to salary negotiations. Generally I find that this is because they think this is the way they're supposed to behave. They mistakenly think that by appearing to be too compliant or will make them appear weak and that they'll be taken advantage of. You should easily be able to recognise this type of behaviour as candidates in this situation are usually unable to provide any reasonable justification for their demands. In such circumstances you should simply stand your ground. They will more often than not accept that your position is a reasonable one and accept your offer, if they are given the time to consider their options and if they know that it's your final offer.

It is not helpful if a candidate perceives that you are being tight fisted just for the sake it. You may indeed need to be tight fisted about certain items, but it's important that the reasons behind your non-negotiable items are communicated and understood.

> **"Of course we'd love to be able to offer you more, but with the current budget restrictions we have we just can't go any higher than we've already offered you"**

Such language makes people feel that you are genuinely doing your best to hire them and will help a lot in terms of making them conducive to accepting your offer.

You should be wary of the candidate who really inflates their expectations based on future performance. I have usually found such bravado to betray an inflated ego or worse still a dreamer! Any demands for salaries above the prevailing market rate needs to be treated with suspicion, especially if you don't really know the person (i.e. if it's coming from an active candidate). I think the best tactic is to offer market rate with some future potential offering such as bonus or a salary increase as long as some clear, specific and tangible performance targets have been met. You can justify your position by saying something like:

> "Yes, we're happy to pay well for high performance, but we only do so after the results have actually been delivered."

Being able to define the range of salaries on offer in the general market and being able to identify where the candidate's experience/capability fits within that range puts you in a strong position to logically justify your offer. I find this approach gives you the upper hand and takes the personal feelings out of the situation. You are relating experience/capability directly to a defined salary range, thereby making the decisions logic based and pretty easy to explain to a candidate.

> "You are not at the top of our salary range because you have little or no experience of "xyz". If you decide to take our offer and subsequently prove yourself capable of successfully delivering "xyz" within agreed time scales, then we can certainly review your salary again against this scale."

Tip - As an employer you should never feel forced into making an inflated salary offer. The best candidate is the one who will deliver what you need and will fit well with your company culture. They will be the one that you are able to negotiate with in an amicable fashion and you will be happy that they are worth every penny you're paying them. You will be able to negotiate a win–win deal with that person and both parties will be happy with the outcome.

CHAPTER 9: MAKING THE MOST OF THE CLOSING PROCESS

How to ensure a graceful closing

If things are not going well during the negotiation phase and it's obvious that a positive result is not going to be achieved, then it's best to close the process gracefully. Explain why you can't meet the person's demands, what your non-negotiable items are and try to close things out in an amicable fashion wherever possible. The world is getting smaller every day and there is little to be gained in falling out with a candidate during the negotiation process. This is a missed opportunity for many businesses – closing gracefully and in a friendly fashion can reap significant rewards in the future. If somebody got close enough to almost accepting your job offer, then they obviously already have a positive impression of the business. Closing things out in a clearly communicated and positive manner leaves the door open to future possibilities. Sometime in the not too distant future the perfect opening for that candidate may come along. It's short sighted to fall out with somebody that you'd like to hire and you really should avoid it if at all possible. Closing things out in a positive fashion will also make it much more likely that a candidate will refer people to you in the future, especially if they think that there's also a possible future role for them with your business.

When things go well and the person actually does take up a job with you, don't forget to ask them for referrals. They'll obviously be feeling positive about the business and will be highly motivated to try to help you. It's very important to make sure people are asked at this time for any candidate recommendations that may be useful to your business. When going through the offer process, a positively minded candidate knows and understands the strengths and possibilities of the business. This makes them a very good sales person for your business when they are talking to other candidates. Make sure to optimise this time period as people will be genuinely keen to help you add more candidates to your talent pool.

It's very common to find that some candidates may be very close "also-rans" during your hiring process. Those who nearly made it to offer but didn't quite match up to your preferred candidate are worth keeping active in your talent pool. Make sure to explain to them exactly why they didn't make it and exactly how close they came. People's abilities can improve significantly over time. The reason that caused you to decide not to hire a candidate may be irrelevant for a future role. Alternatively they may have gained significantly more expertise or experience in a required area by the time you come back to hiring again in the future. I would always encourage such candidates to keep in touch; indeed it makes sense to encourage any candidates with whom you have a positive interview experience to keep in touch. Such additions to your talent pool can be ready-made solutions waiting for a future problem to arise. Frequently such candidate's circumstances can change and if you've encouraged them to stay in touch they may be back to you when they need to find a new role and you may well have the perfect opening for them in the future.

The flip side of this is to always make sure that you directly and politely communicate a rejection to those whom you know you will never hire. Raising false hope is unforgivable and you should always strive to give quick, honest and direct feedback to those you will not be progressing with. The vast majority of candidates are nothing but grateful for such honesty. Word gets around if you treat candidates in a disrespectful manner and again this part of the process acts as a window into your organisation and culture. You should always take the opportunity to present your business in a positive and professional light. I sometimes find that people are fearful of litigious situations if they are too open and honest about such feedback. A suitable response is one such as:

> **"Upon review of your experience and qualifications we have regrettably decided that we do not have a suitable opening for you. We thank you for your interest and we wish you well in your future career."**

> **"Upon review of your experience and qualifications we have regrettably decided that we do not wish to proceed with your application. We have received applications from other candidates whose experience and qualifications are a closer fit to what we require. We thank you for your interest and we wish you well in your future career."**

If somebody has been rejected after an initial interview you should say something like:

> **"I would like to thank for your recent attendance for interview. While we enjoyed meeting with you and felt that you interviewed well we have decided not to proceed with your application. We have reached this conclusion as we have identified a candidate whose experience and qualifications are a closer fit to what we require. We thank you for your interest and we wish you well in your future career."**

The above notes are perfectly acceptable in an email or a letter when dealing with applicants or those who've had a first interview. If somebody has made it to a second or final interview, a phone call is courteous and respectful. This is particularly so if you want to stay in touch with that person in the future. In order to get the person into your talent pool you need to make a phone call explaining your reasons for not progressing and assuring them that they will be under consideration for possible future opportunities with your business.

Checking references

The checking of references has become increasingly difficult in these litigious times. Previous employers are frequently reluctant to make negative comments for fear of legal implications. At other times people are afraid to say too much in case you try to sue them for making a positive recommendation of a candidate that subsequently doesn't work out. A lot of employers tend to merely provide confirmation of basic details such as employment dates and position held. Because of this you need to have your wits about you when conducting reference checks. Don't palm it off as some menial task that's just a box ticking exercise. If you're going to go to the effort of checking references then you need to ensure that it's done properly and it needs to be done by somebody who has a reasonably detailed understanding of what the job role actually requires.

It's very important that reference calls are approached in an open minded and thorough manner. Do not lazily go through the motions, as you will be very likely to miss any hints or warning signs. Your aim is to get the person giving the reference to open up and give some honest feedback on the person. It's a good idea to explain the impressions of the candidate that you have already formed during interviews. It's also a good idea to go into detail about what you want the candidate to deliver for you. A genuine positive referee will explain how they feel the person may perform in such a situation and will be able to freely give examples of how the candidate has been successful for them in similar situations. You shouldn't expect a reference to make a decision for you in terms of hiring or not hiring a person. You are using the process to verify that the opinion that you have formed about the candidate is correct. Remember it's your decision to hire the person and the reference check is merely another quality control step to verify your decision or to prevent you from making a hiring mistake. All too often I've seen situations where hiring managers will say things like: "I'm really not sure about this candidate but let's check their references and if they're positive then let's hire them."

In effect this type of approach is a cop-out. Being afraid to make a positive decision themselves they pass the responsibility onto somebody else. This type of approach should ring alarm bells and suggests that the hiring manager is not really sure what they're after, but they're prepared to hire a candidate because somebody else will make good general comments about them.

> **Tip** – if a candidate gives you a reference letter, always ask for the contact details of the person quoted in the letter. You always need to verify that the person actually wrote the letter and is happy to recommend the candidate. It's so easy to produce fake letters that you should always make it your business to verify that they are genuine.

Things to do before calling a reference

Step 1

Verify that the person you're calling is a suitable and responsible person to give a reference. It's a common trick for candidates to get a reference from a peer or friend and to inflate the person's title to make it look like they are more senior within the organisation. When making a reference call always ask the person directly – what's your role? Did this candidate work directly for you? You can verify the person's job title by searching online or even by contacting the company – just contact reception and say I've been given "xyz" name as a reference –could you please verify their role within the company.

Step 2

Always arrange a time to call a reference; don't just call out of the blue. When speaking with the referee always make sure to let the person know it's confidential and that their opinion will be used as part of your decision-making process but that their opinion is just a part of the process and that it's ultimately your decision. Referees don't like to feel that they're preventing somebody from getting a job. Generally speaking they have a moral obligation to advise you if there's a genuine reason for not hiring somebody. The legalities of such situations are vague at best, so again use the facts and information that you've been able to gather to make an informed decision.

Timing of reference checks

It's inappropriate to check references before you commence offer discussions. If you've made a final decision and you're looking to verify your decision making criteria that's a good time to check references. If you're unsure about somebody, for whatever reason, you can of course check references, but you must explain this and that you're looking for some feedback to assist your final decision, not actually make it for you. As an employer you have the discretion to hire or not to hire somebody within the bounds of the law. Use your selection process, including reference checks, to make a final decision on who you hire based on evidence and fact.

It's good practise to only check references once it's been decided that an offer is to be made. The offer can be made subject to the receipt of satisfactory references. If you wish to check references before an offer is made you must highlight this to the candidate. I would strongly advise that in any situation where you are unsure of a candidate you explain that reference checks are part of the overall decision-making process and are conducted for all candidates. It is not a good idea to give the impression that you have decided not to hire somebody solely on the basis of a reference check. You must explain that the reference check is part of your overall decision-making process.

It's worth bearing in mind that if in doubt you can always make a conditional offer - you do have the right to withdraw the offer if your specified conditions are not met – this might be based on reference checks, medical checks, background checks, security clearance, right to work, etc. If in doubt its best to seek legal advice to ensure you're not violating any discrimination laws. As long as you are not discriminating against a candidate in some unfair way and you are following a fair decision-making process in line with your business needs, you will be fine – you are allowed to make a decision based on the needs of your business. You can include a term in your offer that any offer is subject to certain criteria such as a successful background check or passing a drugs test or a medical.

Making the reference call

I find the initial reaction of the person giving the reference can be quite telling. If they immediately start chatting about the person and are open and communicative then generally that's quite an encouraging sign. Hesitation or nervousness on their part can be very telling. If you remain unconvinced and feel their feedback was not as open as it could be then alarm bells should be ringing for you.

Generally the only way you can be really sure about a reference is if you know the person who's providing the reference. Unfortunately most of the time you don't know the person so most reference checks really just serve as another possible indicator of the potential suitability of the candidate. If you're unsure about offering a role or not, you can of course ask for references explaining that it's a requirement prior to any final decision and offer being made. Top performers generally have no problem with referees being contacted, as long as it doesn't prematurely alert a current employer that they are looking to leave. You can only seek a formal reference from a current employer with express permission and only after a formal offer has been issued.

> **Tip** – some good questions to ask a reference are:
>
> - Are you aware of any reasons why I should not hire this person?
>
> - Is there anything else you think I should know about the person?
>
> - If you had the chance would you re-hire this person in the future?

Failure to disclose something that would prevent you from hiring a candidate is morally unacceptable from any referee that you might talk to. Legally there are no guarantees – which is why most people are really only prepared to give positive references or to merely confirm employment dates. If you're struggling to get a positive reference about a candidate then this should raise a red flag with you.

The ethics of Social Media employer checks

I see nothing wrong with a basic Internet search to verify the existence or absence of any potential red flag issues. If a person is happy to post publicly available content then anyone is perfectly entitled to find and read or look at such content. Any such content can give you an indication of potential areas that require further investigation and by this I mean through interview questioning or via reference checking. It's not advisable to use any such material as the basis of forming a final judgement about a candidate as that would discriminatory. The best way I can summarise the issue is to say – how would you feel if you hired somebody who turned out to be a problematic employee and warning signs were in evidence all over the Internet and would be easily found by anyone that carried out a basic online search? Warning signs can be things like derogatory postings on social media sites or online forums. Such things are not a reason in themselves to not hire somebody but they are possible indicators of patterns of behaviour which could be problematic and are therefore worthy of further investigation.

Current legislation and thinking regarding social media content and its use during the recruitment process is a topic of much debate with little or no hard and fast rules. Various Internet tools including social media can be used to assess or verify the following issues:

- Is the person who they say they are?

- Do they have the experience and qualifications that they claim to have?

- Have they actually had the responsibility they claim and have they achieved what they say they have?

I would recommend that social media be primarily used to verify facts about a person and to make sure that they are genuinely who they claim to be. I don't recommend its use to try to gain some deeper insights into a person's character or competence, as that type of online information is often not verifiable. That type of information needs to be gleaned via your interviewing and reference check process. By way of example, you could use the following information to investigate further and to seek further clarification or verification of the following facts:

- You find online postings by a candidate on a site discussing how to go about faking educational qualifications.

- You are reviewing a CV from an overseas candidate and you want to understand a bit more about the companies they've worked for so you do some online searching. You can find no trace or evidence of one of more companies that the person claims to have worked for.

- You receive a copy of a training certificate that appears to be a fake. You take a look online to search for examples of what a real certificate looks like and you discover that what has been sent to you is indeed a fake.

- You receive a CV with a person's name quoted as a reference. You do a search online and find the person does indeed work for the company, but is not the Managing Director as claimed, but is actually working at a much lower level in the organisation.

- You receive a CV from a candidate who claims a significant achievement that seems very impressive for somebody at their job level. A LinkedIn search of other employees at the same company shows somebody else has actually mentioned that they achieved the exact same thing.

All of these items would be classed as warning signs that warrant further investigation. This should be done through cross examination at interview, verification of qualifications or reference checking.

In conclusion, as an employer you have the discretion to hire or not to hire somebody within the bounds of the law. You use your selection process, including reference and background checks, to make a final decision on who to hire, based on your judgement of evidence and fact. Make sure your hiring decisions are based on who is best to do the job, in line with your specific business needs. Following this process will keep you on the right side of the law. When hiring for myself I always go about the process with the mindset that I would be happy to explain the decision-making process to anybody. I would always feel confident that I can explain the rationale behind the decision to any third party.

CHAPTER 10: SUMMARY - MAKING IT HAPPEN WITH THE TEN KEY STEPS IN YOUR ACTION PLAN

Step 1

Write a clear, concise job specification, making sure to get input from all the relevant stakeholders.

Step 2

Define your person specification to ensure potential new hires fit with your company culture.

Step 3

Write a marketable job advert based on your job and person specification. Make sure you use a job title that will make sense to potential candidates.

Step 4

Define your active candidate sourcing strategy and start advertising straight away.

Step 5

Make full use of your network of suppliers, customers, employee and ex-employee referrals, etc. to identify potential passive candidates. Check back with previous candidates from your talent pool.

Step 6

Review all CVs against your key factors Do so in one sitting and spend an hour creating your short-list. Prepare to interview your short-list of no more than six candidates.

Step 7

Conduct your interviews, making sure to get the most out of the process. Close out properly with any unsuccessful candidates.

Step 8

Manage the offer process to a successful resolution; always check references and never take things at face value.

Step 9

Manage the closing process in a positive and communicative manner with all unsuccessful candidates. Make sure that the door is left open where appropriate.

Step 10

Develop a long term proactive sourcing approach to ensure you fill as many future roles as possible from your talent pool of suitable and interested candidates.

HIRE WITHOUT RECRUITMENT AGENCIES

Printed in Great Britain
by Amazon.co.uk, Ltd.,
Marston Gate.